GIRLS' LIFE MAGAZINE

GL

THE GIRLS' LIFE
BiG BOOK OF QUIZZES
your secret self revealed!

Edited by
Kelly White

Illustrated by
Frank Montagna

Scholastic Inc.
New York • Toronto • London • Auckland • Sydney
Mexico City • New Delhi • Hong Kong • Buenos Aires

ISBN: 0-439-44979-0

Copyright © 2003 by Girls' Life Magazine.

Design: Mark Neston

Illustrations: Frank Montagna/www.artscounselinc.com

All rights reserved. Published by Scholastic Inc.

12 11 10 9 8 7 6 5 4   4 5 6 7 8/0

Printed in the U.S.A.

First Scholastic printing, May 2003

Contents

What's Up?   1

Chapter 1: Got Attitude?   3

Chapter 2: Buddy System   25

Chapter 3: Boy, Oh, Boy!   43

Chapter 4: Cool with School   65

Chapter 5: The Popularity Myth   85

Chapter 6: Get a Grip   99

See Ya!   123

What's Up?

Do you know who you are? Of course, you do! You're Sally or Cyndi or Emma or Shana, you have brown hair with reddish streaks, and you absolutely *love* pepperoni pizza and chocolate milk shakes. But, do you *really* know yourself...deep down?

Do you know where your loyalties lie? Do you know if you have a truly positive outlook on life? Do you know why you and your best friend get along *so* superbly, or what kind of boy makes your heart skip a beat? Hmmm....

That's what this book is all about—it's full of get-to-know-the-*real*-you quizzes, quizzes...and *more* quizzes! So you can test your You IQ! No studying required. Just break out your No. 2 pencil, and start circling away to get in touch with the real you.

Oh, and there's more. Like, did you know that the day you were born, the way you sign your name, and even your favorite color reveal secret clues about you? Well, what are you waiting for? Put yourself to the test—you'll have fun uncovering all sorts of stuff about you-know-who!

Karen

Karen Bokram
Editor-in-Chief, *GL*

Got Attitude?

Attitude is a state of mind, a way of carrying yourself, a feeling, a powerful thing. In fact, your day-to-day attitude is a major part of your personality. It can make the difference in how you feel about yourself and the world around you. Just like a positive outlook can help you overcome a challenge—a negative attitude can lead to missed opportunities, missed friendships, and a whole lot of misunderstandings. What does your attitude say about you? Find out! And learn how to use your attitude to your advantage.

Do You Have a Positive Outlook?

A positive attitude can open the door to more friendships and better relationships. It can also increase the likelihood of success in whatever you do. Find out whether you have too much 'tude, not enough 'tude, or just the right amount of 'tude!

1. Your b-ball team is playing in the championship game against your school's biggest rival. During the team huddle, you suggest everyone chant:

  a. your patriotic school song (dull but traditional).

  b. "Crush them! Beat them! Win!"

  c. "Together!" and slap one another's hands.

2. When your mom suggests a night out on the town, just the two of you, your reply is along the lines of:

  a. "Great! How about dinner and a movie?"

  b. "Yeah, I guess. Going out with my mother is *not* exactly what I had in mind."

  c. "OK. But could I invite some friends over tomorrow?"

3. Volleyball tryouts are this week. When your BFF asks if you think you'll make the JV team, you:

  a. answer, "I'd better. The JV uniforms are so stylin'."

  b. say, "I've been working really hard all week, so I hope so!"

  c. laugh and respond, "Yeah, right! My chances of making JV are about as good as going to the Olympics."

4. It's your very first day of yoga class. As you balance in the tree pose, your yoga-loving friend compliments you on what great shape you're in. You respond:

  a. by falling out of position, pinching an inch, and pointing out all your flaws.

  b. with a confident, "I know!"

  c. by thanking her and returning the compliment.

5. After 45 agonizing minutes of waiting in line to ride the new roller coaster, you're the only one in your group the ticket collector takes aside. When he measures you against the five-foot clown to determine your height, he points out that, sorry, you're not tall enough. So, you:

a. smile and announce to the crowd that it's merry-go-round time for you.

b. feel a bit sorry for yourself, but reassure your buds that you really don't mind waiting by the exit.

c. whine. *Hello?* Did the height-police not notice your vertically challenged friend wearing platforms? When he doesn't budge, you pout to your pals until they surrender and abandon the upside-down super-loopy coaster with you.

6. Your best bud suggests catching the new scary flick this Friday. You know you'll get freaked out—plus, she *always* picks which movie you're going to see. So, you:

a. shrug and say that sounds OK, hoping she receives your telepathic message that you're not thrilled with going to see another thriller.

b. give her a cold look and tell her you have other plans— which you actually had some say in.

c. respond, "Since you picked the last three movies, I'd like to vote on this one."

7. You and one other friend from your swim team are invited to a fellow team member's party. Your host doesn't go to your school, and chances are you won't know most of her guests. In a pow-pow with your friend who's also invited, you say:

a. "Let's go! We'll make it fun, and her friends might be really cool."

b. "Why bother going?"

c. "Let's make an appearance for an hour, and if we don't like it, we can always bolt."

8. **When your history teacher introduces the chapter on Greece, you:**

   a. sarcastically announce loud enough for the back row to hear, "Oooh, this should be exciting!"

   b. say, "Hopefully, it will be better than the chapter about Egypt."

   c. pull out your notebook, grab a pen, and gear up to take notes. Hopefully, you'll learn more about those gorgeous islands with the black sand.

9. **When your English teacher gives you a B instead of the A you anticipated on your Shakespeare report, you:**

   a. deal with it. After all, she knows best because she's the teacher.

   b. read and re-read her comments. You vow to take her suggestions into account for your next book report.

   c. mutter about how unfair she is, walk out of class, and stuff your paper in the trash.

10. **After your brilliant sister brings home yet another Great Scholar Award, which your parents prominently display on the dining room table, you:**

    a. congratulate her, but feel a slight twinge of jealousy.

    b. plan a party in her honor.

    c. stomp out of the room, whining about how you can never live up to her talent, and profess that your parents love her more than you.

Scoring

Total up your points, and then read on to see what your answers reveal about you.

1.	a. 1	b. 3	c. 2		6.	a. 1	b. 3	c. 2
2.	a. 1	b. 3	c. 2		7.	a. 1	b. 3	c. 2
3.	a. 3	b. 1	c. 2		8.	a. 3	b. 2	c. 1
4.	a. 3	b. 2	c. 1		9.	a. 2	b. 1	c. 3
5.	a. 1	b. 2	c. 3		10.	a. 2	b. 1	c. 3

10–16 Points: THE CHEERLEADER

You are a true optimist with a positive, open-minded attitude that lets you have tons of fun and get along with lots of different types of people. That's great! Just make sure you don't let yourself be taken advantage of, or hide your true feelings for the sake of always being so positive.

Sometimes, an over-the-top happy 'tude can seem forced, fake, and even annoying at times. It can also prevent you from dealing with tough issues and feelings that are important to address. Rose-colored glasses are wonderful to wear, just don't let them get in your way when you have something else to say.

17–23 Points: THE BALANCED ONE

You've got a perfectly in-tune 'tude! You're on middle ground—way to go! You have a knack for making the best of any situation. You allow yourself to be positive and open-minded about most things, but you're able to acknowledge and accept your true feelings.

You don't fake that you're oh-so happy when you're actually bummed or disappointed, and you don't expect to be the top dog in all that you do either. Having a positive, yet balanced, attitude is awesome.

24–30 Points: THE GRUMBLER

You have a hard time thinking about things, including yourself, in a positive light. For you, the glass always seems half empty, and sometimes you hurt other people's feelings, or bring them down with your cutting remarks. You don't have to hide your feelings—just convey them in a diplomatic manner, or as fairly and nicely as you can. Try to see the good qualities in others, and yourself, too, and the possibilities for fun will increase for you.

Some things, while seemingly negative, *do* actually work out for the best. Make the most of things, despite the fact that stuff won't always go your way. You'll find yourself a much happier person, and other people will be much more willing to hang out with you as a result.

GET IN A GOOD 'TUDE MOOD

Here are eight ways to jump-start a positive attitude!

1. Gather a group of your friends and bond over chick flicks with cookie dough and sundaes.

2. Go for a run, hop on your skateboard, or take part in other physical activities that will get your adrenaline pumping.

3. Keep a folder of some of your favorite achievements, and flip through it during moments of self-doubt.

4. Call a pal you've lost touch with—just to say hi and catch up.

5. Do something artistic, like taking photographs, sketching, painting, or penning a poem.

6. Do something for someone else. Volunteer at a soup kitchen, bake brownies for a sick bud, or read to a younger sib.

7. Got a pup? Toss around the Frisbee, take your dog for a walk, or just cuddle.

8. Blast your favorite song, and dance around your bedroom.

What's Your Gotta-Have-Fun Style?

Want to have fun? Figure out your gotta-have-fun style, and you'll never be bored again. Turn your life from blah to hurrah! Next time you catch a case of the snores or can't decide what you want to do, do something totally different—based on your gotta-have-fun style.

1. **When it comes to fashion, how would you describe your favorite look?**

a. Casual, like jeans and a faded T-shirt.

b. Neat and sweet, like flowery dresses and pretty sandals.

c. Practical, like your cargo pants— because you can stuff just about anything in all those pockets.

d. Attention-getting, like a hot pink top paired with purple camouflage pants.

2. **Which of the following foods makes your mouth water the most?**

a. A chocolate milk shake with tons of candy bar bits mixed in.

b. A mixed greens salad, and a yogurt parfait for dessert.

c. Fresh corn-on-the-cob, dripping with butter.

d. Pizza—and not just the standard pepperoni. You like yours with gourmet fixin's.

3. **A boy you like wants to plan the ideal Saturday afternoon. Where should the two of you go?**

a. No farther than the bean-bag chairs in your family room. Watching DVDs and playing video games sounds perfect.

b. To the mall, of course. He won't mind waiting while you shop.

c. Rock climbing. You've been dying to go.

d. To the fastest, most stomach-churning roller coaster at the local amusement park—and be ready to ride it *at least* five times.

4. **What's your hair-wear vibe?**

a. Huh? Just lather, rinse, and repeat. No hair accessories necessary.

b. You braid, crimp, straighten or twist your hair into a different style nearly every day of the week. You're especially fond of your huge assortment of barrettes, clips, holders, and headbands.

c. All you need is a ponytail holder. Pull your hair up out of your face and go!

d. You go crazy experimenting with temporary paint-on/wash-out hair color—you live for pizzazz.

5. **What's your ideal Friday night?**

a. Hanging out in your room and getting into a good book.

b. Giving yourself a pedicure.

c. Going camping with your BFF.

d. Going for a ride with your big brother. You and your dog both like sticking your heads out the window to catch the breeze as your older brother drives.

6. **What's your worst nightmare scenario?**

a. Your mom demands that you sacrifice your after-school TV routine to "get some fresh air."

b. You arrive at your cousin's party and discover that another girl is wearing the same dress as you.

c. You get whacked in the thumb by a stray ball on the tennis court, and then find out you'll have to wear a cast and put away your racquet for the rest of the season.

d. Your folks choose a family vacation in a dull little cabin in a dull little town, and there's nobody your age in sight.

7. **How do you feel about loud, pounding thunderstorms?**

a. You can take 'em or leave 'em.

b. They terrify you—plus, rain makes your hair frizz up.

c. You find them fascinating.

d. They're totally thrilling—you love to sit out on your porch and watch lightning explode in the sky.

8. **If you were stranded on an island and could take one thing, which of the following would you take?**

a. The hammock tied between some trees in your backyard.

b. A light, fresh fragrance.

c. A wide-brimmed baseball cap to keep your hair out of your face.

d. Blue cotton-candy.

> ## Scoring
> Review your answers, and total up how many of each letter you selected. Then, look up the letter that you chose most to see what your answers reveal about you.

Mostly A's: Your Fun Style is **VERY VEGGED OUT**

You're all about maxing and relaxing. That's cool. Taking time to chill is healthy. You work hard at school, at after-school sports, and at everything else you do, so recharging your batteries is crucial. Just keep in mind, though, that there's a difference between getting the rest you need and being lazy.

If you find yourself eating too much, sleeping a lot, or feeling generally tired, it's time to work your veg-out vibe in a new way. Chill out more creatively! Why not rev up your brain by trying stuff that'll enrich you? Rent a foreign flick— and actually read the subtitles. Write your autobiography for fun—record all the important events you've experienced so far. Then, write down your hopes and dreams for the next five, ten, or twenty years. Just think what a blast it could be in the future to look back and see which of your dreams came true. Illustrate your life story with photos, drawings, newspaper clippings, whatever best suits your bio.

Mostly B's: Your Fun Style is **GORGEOUSLY GLAM**

You're a fashionista to the core. Your fun style celebrates your inner goddess. But why confine yourself to the same ol' mall trip? If you've been dying to venture into vintage fashion, go for it. Hit thrift stores, consignment shops, and yard sales. The fun and funky pickin's are plentiful—and cheap.

Speaking of cheap fashion—how about *free* fashion? Throw a cast-offs party with your buds. Here's how: Everybody in your crew should dig through their closets and pull out five items they've outgrown or no longer want. Each piece of clothing should be in good condition and shouldn't be totally weird or out of style—you know, everything should be somebody's idea of cool. Then have your crew over to the house, form a big circle, and pull out all the clothes—then it's time to mix, match, and trade.

Mostly C's: Your Fun Style is **AWESOMELY ADVENTUROUS**

You rule as queen of the forest—and the lake, the beach, and your own backyard. You dig being outside from morning to night. You love any and all outdoor sports, and you're constantly on the move—running, riding your bike, climbing rocks and trees—until you're completely pickled.

A fresh athletic buzz can expand your mind and work out your bod in all sorts of cool, new ways. Be on the lookout for those opportunities—why not spend an afternoon fishing with your grandpa? You'll learn a new skill while spending quality time with one of your favorite people. Tag along to your mom's cardio kickboxing class—upper cuts and roundhouse kicks could be just the change of pace you need.

Mostly D's: Your Fun Style is **WILD AND CRAZY**

Your love of life is intense, and you soak up fun experiences full-on. There are so many exciting possibilities every day, in every way, for you to exercise the curiosity that makes you so energetic, fun, and alive! Resolve to try one new food a week—if you've never tried an avocado, go for it! Pretty soon your buds—who, for sure, admire your amazing go-for-it spirit—will want to join in on the taste-testing.

And, hey, why not learn a foreign language, like Italian? Try a cropped new haircut? How about burning a mixed CD of the wackiest, weirdest songs of all time (in your opinion), then duping it and giving copies to all your friends? The sky's the limit, because when you let that impressive imagination of yours loose, there's no end to the unique activity ideas you'll come up with!

Where Do You Fall in the Chinese Zodiac?

According to ancient Chinese tradition, the year you were born sets up certain energies in your life that influence your personality. Check out the following guide to find your sign, then read your personality profile. You can also check out the signs of your younger and older sibs and cousins.

Rabbit

If you were born in 1987, you have a gentle personality. When your siblings or friends are fighting, you're always the peacemaker. You have an optimistic outlook on life and you work hard on self-improvement. You are careful to eat the right foods and to get enough exercise. No fad diets for you! You're into getting proper nutrition.

Dragon

If you were born in 1988, you can be very demanding. You expect a lot from other people, and you don't handle disappointment well. You are a perfectionist who takes love, work, and school very seriously. Try not to let things stress you out too much! Just remember how important it is to have fun!

Snake

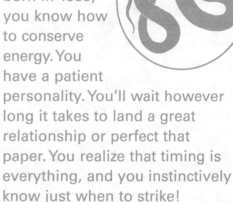

If you were born in 1989, you know how to conserve energy. You have a patient personality. You'll wait however long it takes to land a great relationship or perfect that paper. You realize that timing is everything, and you instinctively know just when to strike!

Horse

If you were born in 1990, you are open and honest with everybody you meet. Sometimes, this can get you in trouble because you are so trusting! You have a kind spirit and a warm energy. Your friends adore you because you are eager to help them out, and you are great at solving problems. Your advice is always on target.

Sheep

If you were born in 1991, you can be shy and removed from the social world. You're not ambitious about becoming the most popular kid at school. You're more interested in creating things, and you are drawn to music, painting, and creative writing. Sometimes you need to learn how to stand up for yourself more because you can be a little too laid-back!

Monkey

If you were born in 1992, you are a social butterfly. You draw energy from other people, and you tend to get bummed if you have to be alone. You are the type of person who would make a great school president or captain of your favorite sports team. People enjoy your funny jokes and your outgoing personality. You are a pleasure to be around.

Rooster

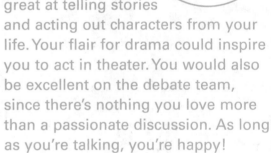

If you were born in 1993, you love to flirt and to entertain an audience. You are great at telling stories and acting out characters from your life. Your flair for drama could inspire you to act in theater. You would also be excellent on the debate team, since there's nothing you love more than a passionate discussion. As long as you're talking, you're happy!

Dog

If you were born in 1994, you have a cheerful and affectionate personality. You always look on the bright side of life, and you spread positive energy. If a friend is feeling down, you can be relied upon to offer a snappy joke or comment that will instantly lift her spirits. You are sensitive to those in need and are generous with your time and money.

Pig

If you were born in 1995, you have an eccentric and quirky style. You insist on doing things your own way, in your own time. If someone wants to be your friend, she will have to take time to get to know you, because you are very complex! You're not a big social climber, preferring instead to hang out with close buds who will remain loyal to you for a long time.

Rat

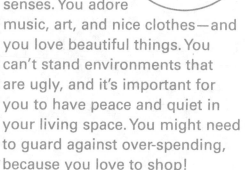

If you were born in 1996, you love to indulge your senses. You adore music, art, and nice clothes—and you love beautiful things. You can't stand environments that are ugly, and it's important for you to have peace and quiet in your living space. You might need to guard against over-spending, because you love to shop!

Ox

If you were born in 1997, you tend to be a homebody. You'd much rather read a book or play on your computer than deal with a big group of people. You are a hard worker, and yours is one of the few signs that actually enjoys receiving homework! You don't mind doing research or writing reports because you are great at analyzing things.

Tiger

If you were born in 1998, you are restless and dramatic. You are always on the move, wandering from one adventure to another. You tend to change friends every few months because you get bored if you have to hang out with the same people all the time. You find it hard to focus on just one thing because you are always entertaining new options.

How Motivated Are You?

Now that you know your gotta-have-fun style, it's time to buckle down and get serious. Breaking bad habits or getting around to all the stuff on your to-do list should be a top priority. Is it? Take this quiz to find out if you're a goal-oriented girl and if you have the stick-to-it savvy it takes to meet those goals.

1. Your jeans have been feeling tight, so you've vowed to watch what you eat. Your buds want to hit the burger joint for a feast. How do you deal? You:

a. stay home and resentfully munch on carrot sticks as you think of your friends enjoying their pig-out session.

b. order a low-fat grilled chicken sandwich. When your BFF offers to share her fries with you, though, you can't resist grabbing a handful.

c. give in to temptation and eat all the fattening junk you want. Your healthful eating plan lasted a whole day— that's long enough.

d. say, "Jumbo-size fries, please!"

2. Your grades could use a lift this semester, so you make up your mind to spend an extra hour each night on your homework. The problem is your little sister. Whenever you're trying to study, she bursts into the room you both share and makes tons of noise. She ruins your concentration and makes it hard to refocus. How do you handle this?

a. You ask your mom to pop in a DVD for your sister, so you can get your work done.

b. You put on some headphones while she chatters away. You're still distracted, but at least you have a little background music.

c. You give up on the books as soon as she blasts into the room and tell yourself you'll try to work tomorrow.

d. You get really angry and scream at her. Now you're in no mood to study.

3. Your room is a mess. You haven't made your bed in days, your clothes and CDs are everywhere—and could that be a petrified slice of pepperoni pizza stuck to the rug? Things are beyond gross, so you do a massive cleanup and promise yourself you'll maintain order forever. How does your room look a week later?

a. It's still spotless.

b. It looks pretty good—but you could tackle that growing pile of clutter on your desk.

c. Your stuff is all over the place again, but you'll straighten it up...later.

d. It's totally disgusting. So what? You're naturally a slob.

4. You love the look of long, manicured fingernails. You decide you want some, so you:

a. stop nibbling your digits immediately. You're fired up to grow them out perfectly.

b. make an appointment to get fake nails at a salon. That way, you can get the look without actually going through the effort of growing out your nails.

c. start growing out your nails, but get kind of bored with the whole concept in a couple of days and quit.

d. just keep daydreaming. You don't have the discipline to take care of long nails.

5. You and your BFF have made a pact to start an exercise program. Every day after school, you promise you'll go for a run— even if it's cold outside. After a while, your BFF starts missing some workouts. What do you do? You:

a. keep jogging each day, whether your BFF joins you or not.

b. ask your BFF if she wants to cut back your runs from five days a week to only two or three.

c. decide to put off the entire plan until spring, when the weather will be nicer.

d. ditch the workouts for good.

6. Admit it—you're addicted to gum. But, last week, you caught a glimpse of yourself in the mirror mid-chomp, and it was *not* a pretty sight. So, you decide to quit cold turkey. Problem is that your friends are always breaking out the Juicy Fruit—and the cotton-candy-flavored Bubble Yum at the drugstore checkout is calling your name. How do you cope with the temptation? You:

a. just keep picturing that image of yourself in the mirror—it will remind you how unclassy gum chewing can really look.

b. beg your crew not to chew in your presence, and avoid candy counters at all costs.

c. sneak a piece of gum now and then—just to satisfy your urge.

d. give in, and start chewing twice as much gum as before. Maybe the more you chew, the sooner you'll get sick of it.

7. You're always short of cash, so you've decided to save half of your allowance each week. Trouble is, now your fun-funds are limited. Your friends keep sabotaging your money-saving plan by inviting you to the movies and the mall. What can you do?

a. Stay strong. Explain to your buds that you really want to achieve your saving goals—suggest cool, free activities you can do together instead.

b. Go to the mall with your pals, but stick to your budget.

c. Feel free to spend as much as you'd like every once in a while—you deserve a treat.

d. Chuck the whole financial responsibility thing. You only live once.

8. You make a resolution to give more of your time to people in need, so you volunteer at a local nursing home. You really love visiting with the elderly people who live there. Still, you have to miss all of your school's weekend basketball games because of your schedule. That seems pretty unfair. So, now what?

a. You remind yourself that you're the one who committed to volunteering. You have no reason to complain.

b. You can't really change your schedule now without looking selfish. So, when you're talking with the supervising nurse, you casually mention the games you're missing, and hope she'll suggest that you adjust your schedule.

c. You skip a few visits to the nursing home to catch some games. You're a volunteer— what are they going to do, fire you?

d. This situation is unbearable. You quit volunteering, and think of your own enjoyment first and foremost.

9. You just got a brand-new computer, and it's really cool— but it's so complicated to set up. You vow to figure out how to make it work all by yourself, and to keep learning amazing new ways to use it. You:

a. practically memorize the instruction booklet and keep at it until you're making iMovies like a pro.

b. play around with it for a while, but get frustrated and decide to watch a DVD—you'll try again later.

c. ask your mom to set it up for you. If you want it to do more stuff later on, she'll just have to help you again.

d. leave the computer in its box. You don't understand how to operate the thing, so no matter how awesome it is, it's going back to the store.

10. You really want to negotiate a later bedtime on school nights. Your mom says you'll have to prove you're mature enough to handle it before she'll say OK. You're determined to be more responsible in general. Things are going great until your crush, Chad, calls you one night. You're talking up a storm, when you happen to glance at the clock— it's an hour past your bedtime on a school night, and your parents know you're on the phone! You've ruined your chances—how do you handle it?

a. You tell Chad you'll catch him in school tomorrow, then quickly explain your mistake to your mom.

b. You talk to Chad a few more minutes, hang up, and pray that your mom thinks you hung up an hour ago.

c. When your mom asks if you were on the phone past your bedtime, you adamantly deny that it's true.

d. When your mom confronts you about the late-night phone time, you completely freak out on her.

Mostly A's: You've got DETERMINATION AND DESIRE

Determination—you've got loads of it! You're likely to succeed at whatever you set out to do because you make strong decisions to do so. Determination is really all about staying calm and knowing what you want. You're willing to work hard to accomplish your goals. You're committed—and you won't easily fall apart under stress or temptation. You're really good at figuring out exactly what you need to do to make positive changes—you focus on the details. Congrats on being all you can be.

Remember, you don't need to be perfect, though—nobody is. If you do happen to veer from your plan, don't beat yourself up—you're only human. Also, don't go it alone. Your determination might be strong enough to move mountains, but it's totally cool to ask your friends for help when you need it. They care about you and should be happy to lend you a hand.

Mostly B's: You're MOSTLY MOTIVATED

You've got good intentions, for sure. You really want to accomplish things, even when they're a bit challenging. But you tend to run out of steam after pursuing stuff for a little while. Don't feel bad—you can definitely juice up your motivation.

To start, try a little creative visualization. Imagine yourself looking terrific after you've toned up from regular workouts, and you'll be fired up for that after-school run. Say you've decide to grow out your layered shag so—be sure you really dig that long, swingy hair vibe. If you don't, your growing pains will be such a drag, you'll give up and get a buzz cut. OK, we're kidding about the buzz!

Mostly C's: You've got to ORGANIZE YOURSELF

OK, you're kind of scattered. Your locker tends to be messy, and you can never find what you need *when* you actually need it. That's why you need to get into the groove of organization by putting things in order—keeping things simple. You probably hang on to every scrap of paper from every class because, deep down, you're afraid you'll throw away something really important. To avoid such feelings, take the time to go through all your papers. Throw away what you don't need, and trust your instincts—you already know what's important and what isn't.

Maybe you're scared to straighten up your biology papers. What if you organize them, promise to get a better grade, but then don't do so well? Don't be spooked by the possibility that you'll fail at something—you deserve awesome grades, so just go for them. Spend some time every Sunday night getting your school stuff together for the coming week. Don't put too much pressure on yourself, though—just try, and if you get a B- instead of an A+ in bio, at least you put in a good effort. If you do your best, that's all anyone can ever expect of you.

Mostly D's: You need INSPIRATION

Your focus is funky. In order to meet any goal, you've got to clear up your internal confusion. Prioritizing can help. Prioritizing means ranking what's most important to you and tackling the key stuff first and foremost. What do you want to change most about yourself? Sit down and truly think about it— do you want to be more outgoing? How about making your convictions simple. Start smiling more and saying hi to kids at school you don't know very well. People dig a friendly attitude. You'll quickly find people being friendly back, and you'll soon have more than just a few new buds to hang with.

In terms of inspiration, check out role models who you think have super personalities, and take note of their traits. Let them inspire you— maybe you wish you had your big sister's sense of humor, your mom's generosity, or an athlete's dedication to the sport she trains so hard for. Find your best successes by checking out the qualities you admire most in others, and trying them out in your own way.

HOW TO STAY PSYCHED

You might find that staying psyched on a daily basis is tough. Here are some easy ways to keep going strong until your good intentions are a way of life.

- **BE PRACTICAL.** Make sure your goals fit into your current lifestyle. You can always work gradually toward larger goals. For instance, if you want to learn how to cook, don't offer to bake the perfect birthday cake for your BFF 'til you've got the hang of things.

- **DON'T PREACH.** Never lecture your friends or family. It's great to be proud of your progress, but if you talk too much about it, others tend to pass out from boredom. Or, they get offended and feel like you're telling *them* to shape up. Convictions are personal—this is *your* plan for self-improvement, not anybody else's. So be considerate.

- **RESEARCH YOUR STRATEGY.** Say you want to save half of your allowance each week. Form a battle plan. Grab a piece of paper, and write your goal at the top of the page. Now strategize. Figure out how much money you have now. Write it down. Figure out how much money you'll be saving each week and for how many weeks—set a reasonable goal at first, like a month total (four weeks). Now add up all the money you'll have one month from now, combining what you already have with what you resolve to save. You'll be really psyched to see those dollars add up.

- **GIVE YOURSELF PROPS FOR ALL YOUR HARD WORK.** It's really hard to keep jogging every day after your BFF has hung it up, for example. It's really hard to do anything new at first. You deserve credit for being persistent.

Is Your Number Up?

Numerology is all about discovering your personal energy number. To figure out where your verve vibe falls on a scale from 1 to 9, look at the numbers in the month, date, and year of your birth.

Let's say you were born October 6, 1993. October is the tenth month, so you start with the number 10 (your month of birth). Then add 6 (your day of birth) and 1, 9, 9, and 3 (your year of birth). So you'll be adding 10 + 6 + 1 + 9 + 9 + 3. This equals 38. Keep adding numbers left to right until they reduce down to just a single digit. So, now you would add 3 + 8. This equals 11. Then repeat what you just did, but add 1 + 1. This equals 2. There you have it: 2 would be your personal energy number! After you've reduced your birth date down to your personal energy number, check out the following to see what it means.

1 If your personal energy number is 1, you are an independent person. You don't like others to have control over you, so when your parents give you a list of chores, it really bums you out! You love to stand out in a crowd. You hate homework, chores, and anything that isn't fun!

2 If your personal energy number is 2, you work best with a partner. When studying a difficult course at school, you'll understand things better if you team up with a study buddy. And if you are attending a dance or a party, you like to have somebody at your side. Without a friend nearby, you tend to get nervous sometimes!

3 If your personal energy number is 3, your main motivation is to build and create. You love to make things. You might be involved with crafts and decorating. You could design programs on the computer, or come up with graphics for a web-page. You have a strong imagination and are filled with ambition. You aim to succeed!

4 If your personal energy number is 4, you have a dual personality. There are times when you are extremely social, and other times when you just want the world to leave you alone! Your parents might not always know where you are coming from because your moods can change so quickly. Try to express your feelings in a positive way, and others will soon understand you better.

5 If your personal energy number is 5, you crave constant adventure. You're always climbing that next mountain or planning a new quest. It's not enough for you to just get good grades. You want to earn straight A's! And you're not happy liking just any boy. You want him to be the ultimate Mr. Right! Sometimes you set goals that are a little lofty. You need to learn to slow down and allow things to unfold at their own pace.

6 If your personal energy number is 6, you are best at working within a group. You don't like to be called on in class because you are somewhat shy. But when working on a team project, or creating something with a bunch of people, you are able to be more outgoing. Eventually, you'll need to develop the ability (and nerves) to stand on your own. You can do it!

7 If your personal energy number is 7, you have some interesting theories on life. Mysteries of any sort fascinate

you. You're probably interested in astronomy, psychology, and archaeology. You want your life to be filled with magic. As long as you keep one foot planted firmly on the ground, there's no reason the other part of you can't aim for the stars!

8 If your personal energy number is 8, you are always looking for the logical solution to a problem. You like to measure things and take things apart as you study them. You're good at dissections because you are curious about how things fit together (including anatomy!). You're a natural doctor, engineer, or scientist.

9 If your personal energy number is 9, you have a generous spirit. No matter how much stress you are under, you tend to put your friends and loved ones first. If your mom is feeling down, you try to cheer her up or help her in some way. If a friend is gloomy, you give her a special gift, or make her a CD of her favorite songs. Just don't get so busy looking after everybody else that you forget to take care of yourself!

A Fun Way to Learn More About You

Buddy System

Your pals, your posse, your *compadres*...your gals, your buds, your BFFs.... They're all that and more. And so are you! Find out just what kind of fine friend you are.

Are You a Loyal Friend?

You know you're a great friend. You always share your cheese curls with your BFF at lunch, and whenever she comes to your house, you let her sit on your favorite bean-bag chair. But how *loyal* are you? Find out if you're a forever-to-the-end friend or if you need a few lessons in the loyalty department.

1. **Each night, you e-mail your friends with the latest news about everyone at school. Your BFF lets you know it makes her iffy about ever trusting you with another secret. Hearing her say that hurts your feelings, so you:**

a. e-mail your entire buddy list about your best pal's secret crush on the gym teacher.

b. drop your best friend for your cyber buds because online gossip is your life.

c. realize she might be right and curb the chat about others.

2. **Your friend just got a haircut. She loves it, but you think it's hideous. You:**

a. avoid being seen with her until her hair grows out at least another two inches.

b. kindly suggest she try a different hairstyle next time.

c. do nothing. You don't like the new 'do, but she does. It's her hair, so it's her choice.

3. **Your friend's crush is your lab partner, and he asks you to go to the science fair with him. You:**

a. tell amoeba boy it's a date. Cute boys win over friends every time.

b. hope your friend will understand when you tell her you like microscope man.

c. crush his test tube because you would never cross a friend.

4. **A good friend of yours moved like 10,000 miles away. You keep sending her "miss-you" cards, but she hardly writes back. You:**

a. moan about how you always pick the worst friends and swear she's out of your life.

b. mail her one last card that says, "I hope you're happy in your new home!" Then, vow you'll move on if she doesn't respond.

c. give her more time. She's probably busy adjusting to her new place.

5. **Your best friend sits next to you in history class, and you see her cheating on a quiz. You:**

a. talk to her privately after class about the risks of cheating and offer to help her study for next week's big exam.

b. let her know what you saw and explain that she could have gotten you in trouble. If she had been caught, the teacher would surely have assumed you two were in on that cheating thing together.

c. turn her in to the principal. Cheating should not be tolerated.

6. **You and a gal pal have plans for a makeover/sleepover, but later, you are invited to an awesome party on the same night. Your friend isn't invited, so you:**

a. call your bud at the last minute and tell her you have a whooping cough. You wouldn't miss this party for the world.

b. stick with your original plans and have fun with your friend making face masks and giving each other manicures.

c. dress your friend in camouflage, bring her to the party, and hope the hostess doesn't detect her.

7. **The brainy kid your friends call "Gigabyte Guy" has kind of grown on you. You:**

a. give him a chance because you like his smarts.

b. hang out with him so he can help you pass the math final. Then, move on.

c. ignore him because of your friends' opinions.

8. **Your friend's fourteen-year-old dog dies, and she is devastated. You:**

a. dump all your problems on her to distract her from her grief.

b. rent the *Old Yeller* video for her to watch.

c. listen to her puppy tales with a box of tissues handy.

9. It's 95 degrees outside, and an unpopular girl invites you to swim in her Olympic-size pool. You:

a. go, and discover you both love synchronized swimming. You dive into a great friendship.

b. chill at her pool all summer long, but give her the cold shoulder when school starts.

c. tell her you can't go because chlorine ruins your hair.

10. Your friend wants to be a pop star, but you think she sounds like a sick cow when she sings. You:

a. suggest she take voice lessons to increase her chances of having a career in the spotlight.

b. say, "The only thing musical about you is the fact that you can harmonize with howling dogs."

c. support her dream.

Scoring

Add up your points. Then read on to discover what your answers say about you.

1.	**a.** 1	**b.** 2	**c.** 3		**6.**	**a.** 1	**b.** 3	**c.** 2
2.	**a.** 1	**b.** 3	**c.** 2		**7.**	**a.** 3	**b.** 2	**c.** 1
3.	**a.** 1	**b.** 2	**c.** 3		**8.**	**a.** 2	**b.** 1	**c.** 3
4.	**a.** 1	**b.** 2	**c.** 3		**9.**	**a.** 3	**b.** 1	**c.** 2
5.	**a.** 3	**b.** 2	**c.** 1		**10.**	**a.** 3	**b.** 1	**c.** 2

10–16 Points: You are like **BENEDICT ARNOLD**

For shame! You would turn your back on a friend in a heartbeat. There's this thing called empathy, and you might need to work on developing some. In other words, you should learn to put yourself in other people's shoes. No, you're not going to borrow your best friend's loafers. Pretend for a moment that you are the other person, and imagine how you would want to be treated in a specific situation.

Next time your friend's crush asks you to accompany him to the science fair, for example, think about how you would feel if it were *your* crush who asked out *your* friend. How would that make you feel, and what would you expect your friend to do about it? You would want her to consider your feelings and decline the boy's invite, *right*? Right! And you should give your bud the same consideration. From here on out, vow to put yourself in your pal's place before speaking or taking action.

17–22 Points: You are in **ALL-ABOUT-ME LAND**

You're a fairly loyal friend, but sometimes you tend to think of yourself and that's OK. It's cool to set boundaries so you don't get walked on, but is your me-me-me attitude over the top? Draw the line when it comes to sacrificing your beliefs and values—but also be willing to occasionally bend for a friend.

Friends are forever...if you treat them with respect. Your friend didn't get invited to the party of the century? Show her you're her true-blue, and do a girls' night in—just the two of you. Parties happen all the time, but a BFF can be one in a million. Don't blow it!

23–30 Points: You are **A TRUE BOSOM BUDDY**

You're the kind of friend everyone should treasure. You think of your friends first no matter what. You'd stick up for them through thick or thin. You're there for them when they need you—and even when they don't.

Just be careful not to be taken advantage of. And never, ever compromise your own well-being or convictions just to back up a friend. You offer to help a friend study for an exam, but she wants you to help her improve her cheating skills instead? Say, "No way!" In this case, it's imperative that you stand your ground, even if it means letting your friend down.

What's Your Birth Order?

Are you the oldest in a whole brood of brothers and sisters? Maybe you're the baby, or smack dab in the middle. Knowing the hidden secrets of birth order (where you fit in among your siblings) can help you see yourself in a new light. Birth order says a lot about how you express yourself and how you get along with others. Believe it or not, birth order can even determine what kind of BFF you might be most blissfully matched with.

One and Only

You're an only child? Cool. You're confident and determined. While you don't always feel a need to be surrounded by a bunch of buds (you're really good at entertaining yourself), you do get along best with firstborns because they're highly motivated, like you. After all, they were only children once, too, before their sibs came along, right? However, you tend to butt heads with another only child since you're both *sooo* set in your ways. Your friends might say it can sometimes be hard to get close to you, but it's totally worth it once they do.

Oldest Sister of Sisters

Because you're used to being a nurturing leader, you get along with girls who have older sisters. You're good at giving advice, and you watch your BFF's back like a hawk. Loyalty is very important to you. You can be friends with a girl who's also an oldest sister, but conflicts can creep up—you are both used to being in charge! Compromise, and let your caring nature rule the day.

Oldest Sister of Brothers

You're a great listener and can get people to open up better than almost anyone. Who is your ideal BFF? It probably won't surprise you that a lot of guys think you are just great. Matter of fact, you probably secretly prefer their company to that of other girls. Why? You've been taught to care for and enjoy being with boys. When looking for female friends, try a girl who is an only child. She could be an eager audience for your caring ways.

Middle Girl

You middlers are the most social of any birth-order group. It's no wonder you are friends with so many people. Because you are used to dealing with bossy older sibs and younger ones who hog all the attention, you get along with just about everybody. Just watch out for that tendency to seek out attention and be clingy—you might feel over-looked at home, but you need to be careful not to overwhelm your friends.

Youngest Sister of Sisters

Are you on the swim team, running for student council, and a member of 16 different clubs? Youngest sisters are major entertainers and are used to having an audience. Your friends think you are the life of the party. You are great at sharing your problems with your friends. Seek out older sisters who love to give you the advice you need, or only children who can show you how to be a tad more independent.

Youngest Sister of Brothers

Aren't you the belle of the ball? Not only do you make friends easily, but guys adore you. You'll have to work hard to overcome the jealousy some girls might feel. Look for other younger sisters—they're as lively and interesting as you are.

Do You Give Fab Friend Advice?

If you have parents, homework, or a crush, you've probably turned to your friends for advice! But what happens when *they* are looking for solutions? Are you the go-to guru, or could your friends get better guidance from a fortune cookie? Find out if you should be hosting your own talk show or if you could use a bit of advice when it comes to giving advice.

1. **You dash into the bathroom and find one of your friends leaning against a paper towel dispenser, crying. She just failed a math quiz because her parents argued so loudly last night that she couldn't study. You suggest she:**

a. clamp on some earphones and crank up the tunes next time. It always works for you!

b. not even worry about it—there will be plenty more quizzes before the final exam.

c. talk alone with her math teacher. The teacher might be willing to let your friend retake the quiz or do some extra credit work based on her "extenuating" circumstances.

d. think about the big picture. She'll have to ace the rest of the semester. But, more important, it sounds like her parents might be getting a divorce or something.

2. **Your friend Meghan has a mad crush on Billy, who's president of the drama club. So, she signed up to audition for *The Sound of Music*. You know the only singing she's ever done is in the shower, and auditions are tomorrow. She asks you, "Should I go through with it?" You say:**

a. "Break a leg. You'll do great!"

b. "To audition or not to audition? That is the question."

c. "It's great that you want to be in the musical, but if you haven't been practicing, it might be a better idea to go out for set design."

d. "Ohmigod! Are you serious? You can't even sing the ABC's without your voice cracking twenty-six times. Dude, if you try out, your crush might *never* talk to you."

33

3. **Your friend Kari is getting thinner and thinner. What do you say to her about it?**

a. "Do you have intestinal flu? Because one time I got it and lost, like, a million pounds in one weekend."

b. Nothing. If it's a big deal, someone else will say something to her.

c. "Hey, I am only saying this because I care about you. I'm worried that you've lost weight. You know...in case you want to talk about it."

d. "Ever hear of food? Here, let me introduce you to my friend Mr. Cheeseburger."

4. **Your friend Carmen calls you in a panic. She's going to the dance with *him*, and she just broke the zipper on her dressy dress. Even worse, *he's* going to be at her house in ten minutes. What do you say?**

a. "The same thing happened to me once. I was supposed to meet this cute guy from camp and I was freaking out because I'd gotten lip gloss on my white top. My older sister let me borrow a black shirt and her denim jacket, so it was fine."

b. "Bummer. What are you gonna do?"

c. "Why don't you wear your adorable blue dress instead? After all, he didn't ask the dress to the dance, he asked YOU!"

d. "I told you that dress was cheap—that's why it was so discounted."

5. **You and your BFF Ingrid spent all weekend watching scary movies. It's Sunday night, and Ingrid's home alone. She's totally spooked, and she's called you five times in the last half-hour. You need to get some Z's. When she calls a sixth time—and she will—you're going to:**

a. tell her you're not the Ghostbuster's hotline and you need your beauty rest!

b. let the voice mail pick up—you've had it.

c. suggest she seek out some comic relief and pop in *Shrek* until she falls asleep. It works!

d. tell her she's a stalker-freak for calling you all night long, and then hang up on her.

6. **Your BFF Gina is battling with her friend Amy again. Apparently, Amy won't respond to Gina's calls or e-mails. Gina asks you what she should do. You say:**

a. "Ugh, I hate it when people ignore me! Just do what I always do—ignore them."

b. "I'd rather not be involved. Plus, I don't really know Amy."

c. "I understand what you're going through. Write Amy a little note and tell her you miss her. If we ever get in a tiff, I hope we could get it out in the open like that."

d. "Face it—she's not a good friend. Stop acting like a puppy dog, and move on."

7. **It's test time, and your pal Janelle is failing Spanish. She wants to tell her parents before the *Señora* does but she doesn't know how to break the news. What do you tell her?**

a. "It reminds me of the time I left my new parka at the mall, and I had to tell my mom. She got pretty mad, and for the rest of the winter I had to wear my old coat from the year before."

b. "*No comprendo, mi amiga.*"

c. "Yikes! You should give your parents a heads-up. Ask the teacher about setting up some extra one-on-one tutoring time so your folks know you're trying to pull your grade up for next semester."

d. "What's wrong with you—haven't you been studying?"

8. **Last night, your pal Laurie saw her mom and new stepfather kissing. Laurie is totally grossed out. Your advice?**

a. Tell her you'd freak, too!

b. Ask her for the details.

c. Listen and let her vent. Then, ever so nicely, remind her that her mom's an adult and, well, she just got remarried.

d. *Ew!* Tell her she's grossing you out, too! Then suggest she knock from now on before she enters any room in her house.

Mostly A's: SHALLOW PAL

Where do you go to school? Because there's no "u" in "advice." You have an amazing way of making everyone's personal dilemmas all about you. Whether giving advice isn't your bag or you think your experiences speak for themselves, it's time to shift the spotlight away from yourself a bit and become a more compassionate pal.

It's OK to share your personal experiences if you've had a similar problem—just don't make yourself the center of the solution. *Listen* to what your friend is saying. Chances are, when she's finished, the first thing to pop into your mind will be a similar situation—starring you, of course. Instead of starting right in with that great story of yours, count to ten and really think about what you're about to say. If it's truly constructive and helpful, your first sentence won't start with an "I."

Mostly B's: SPACE CASE

Your friend is asking for your help. Saying to her, "I don't know," or changing the subject is *not* helpful—on any planet. What *is* helpful is a response that shows you were listening and that you care. You don't have to enter *The Twilight Zone* every time your BFF wants your opinion.

Ask her how she feels about the situation or what solutions she's already tried or considered. There's also a chance she doesn't want you to tell her what to do anyway—she might just want to talk about it. So relax and offer reassuring statements like, "I know how you must feel." If she really pushes you for some wise words, by all means, share your thoughts—you just might find you have something helpful to add after all.

Mostly C's: ADVICE DOCTOR

You've got it going on. You're caring, compassionate, and never pass judgment on your friends. You have a great way of making people relax and are able to see things from a different angle. By listening and asking questions, you often guide your friends to the best solution rather than giving them a road map to your own opinions.

You might find your posse lining up in the lunchroom to pour out their problems to you. Just be sure to practice what you preach and avoid getting so wrapped up in other people's problems that you forget to have fun and take care of your own life!

Mostly D's: JUDGE JILL

Tough love is one thing, but what you're dishing out might be more than what your friends want to hear between blows into a tissue. It's great that you have a firm opinion on everything—but that doesn't mean your road is always necessarily the right one.

Why not soften the punch a little bit? Try putting yourself in your BFF's sitch and help her come to her own conclusions. It's OK to share what you would do if confronted with the same dilemma—just don't lay it down like it's the law. And if your friend just wants to talk, let her.

FIVE SECRETS TO GIVING GREAT ADVICE EVERY TIME

Amp up your advice skills by keeping these five ideas in mind. Think of them as advice on giving advice ('cause they are)!

1. **TAKE THE TIME TO REALLY LISTEN.** This is the best way to determine whether your friend really wants your two cents or just needs to talk it out. Most likely, she will explain her situation and ask for your opinion. If you've been listening, it'll be easy to figure out whether she wants you to help her decide the next step, or if she's just looking for a thoughtful ear.

2. **AVOID STARTING SENTENCES WITH "I."** Like, "I think you should..." These types of responses can make your friend feel like you're judging her instead of helping her. Instead, try "If I were in your situation, I might...."

3. **ASK OPEN-ENDED QUESTIONS THAT MAKE HER PONDER.** Here are some examples: "What have you tried already?", "Why do you think that didn't work?", and "What would you like to do but haven't yet tried?"

4. **TRY TO AVOID INSENSITIVE PHRASES.** Like, "Don't worry about it," or "Try to stay busy." These send signals that you're way too cool to be dealing with her small problems. Although you might mean well, the only thing your friend will hear is, "I know better than you do," or "Your problems aren't really significant."

5. **DEVELOP EMPATHY.** This means you're listening so closely that you understand what your friend is feeling and you can share her sadness, fear, or anger. Your grandma might call it, "walking a mile in someone else's shoes." Sure, it sounds sappy, but it really works!

What's Your Dependability Vibe?

Are you afraid to say "no" when your buds ask outrageous favors—and lots of them? Or, are you a goddess of organization who loves a good challenge? Take this quiz to discover your dependability vibe. Then read on for our tried-and-true take on how to boost your count-on-me quotient.

1. **Your BFF Amanda is having a tough time in algebra. You're pulling an A average, so Amanda asks you to help her study. You:**

   a. show up half an hour early with charts, graphs, and sample problems you wrote up for her.

   b. run through some homework assignments with her until she feels more in control of things.

   c. are watching TV when you remember you were supposed to meet her.

2. **You and your buds are cruising the racks at a department store. Everybody loves the same black shoes. The sales girl sees you all admiring them and says, "Tomorrow they go on sale for half off—but we only have size 6," which happens to be your size and nobody else's. You all agree that if you can't all have them,** none of you will have them. The next day:

   a. you've already forgotten all about them. Shoes are a dime a dozen—friendship is forever.

   b. you find yourself still thinking about how cool they are, but a deal is a deal so you're not going to buy them.

c. you slink back to the store and plunk down your cash. You'll only wear them when your buds aren't around.

3. It's 8 a.m. on Monday. Where are you?

a. In homeroom, with your BFF. You two hook up every Monday morning to quiz each other before the weekly vocab test.

b. Hanging at your locker, chatting with your other friends—you've still got time before the first bell rings.

c. Munching your second donut in the kitchen, having lost all track of time.

4. How is your watch set?

a. Five minutes fast. You hate being late to anything.

b. On time. That way, you don't need to rush to get somewhere or waste time by arriving too early.

c. Watch? What watch? Oh, yeah—you accidentally left it in the locker room.

5. It's Friday night, and you're psyched to bust some moves at the school dance. You and your friend decided to go together.

Then, your ultimate crush calls out of nowhere and asks you to join him for pizza instead. Short of cloning yourself, how do you deal?

a. You thank your crush for the invite but let him know you already have plans, and suggest the two of you go for pizza on Saturday instead.

b. You're bummed at the idea of missing the pizza opp, so you call your friend and beg her to let you off the hook. There will be plenty more dances.

c. You blow off the dance and, when your friend asks where you were, you tell her you came down with a cold.

6. Your friend passes you a note that says Jason told her he likes you. But she's not supposed to be telling you because he wants to do it himself. Jason will get mad at her if he finds out she spilled. What do you do?

a. You thank your friend for letting you know and promise not to breathe a word until Jason approaches you.

b. You're about to burst with excitement, so you tell just a couple friends as soon as study hall lets out.

c. You pass Jason a note that says it's way cool he likes you and that you'll be having lunch in the caf around noon, if he's free.

7. **Your best bud is the head of the stage set committee for this year's class play. It's cool, but closer to show time, people get bored and quit the crew. Your friend asks you to do tons of extra work—hang curtains, buy makeup, round up props, you name it. You're exhausted:**

a. but, no way are you going to bail on your bud. You made a commitment, and you're going to honor it, even if you're the last crew member left.

b. so, you nicely tell your friend you're overextended, and ask her to get the drama teacher to figure it out.

c. so, you blow off the scene. Who cares if your friend is left in the lurch? That's her problem. You didn't sign up to head the committee—she did.

8. **Your friend always gets you to braid her hair because you're so good at it. You're getting a little tired of being her personal hairdresser. What do you tell your braided bud?**

a. "I'm going to braid your hair again today, but let's get together at my house this weekend so I can teach you how to braid your own hair. It'll be fun."

b. "I need a break from the braiding. I'll do it for you next week." Then, never do it.

c. "My fingers are getting in more of a twist than your hair, so don't ask me to braid your hair anymore. Got it?"

9. **Your BFF Chloe tells you her folks are getting divorced. She's beyond upset and doesn't want you to tell anybody. You swear you won't. Later that day, another super-close bud asks you point-blank, "Are Chloe's parents splitting up?" Would you tell her?**

a. No. It's Chloe's life and Chloe's business. She'll share it with her other friends when she's ready. For now, you've got to be loyal and keep quiet.

b. Yes. She means well and wants to help Chloe, so there's no harm in her knowing.

c. Yes. You'd crack under the pressure—no matter how important keeping your lips zipped might be, when push comes to shove, you just can't keep a secret.

10. How far in advance do you schedule things on your calendar?

    a. Months—you've got every school dance, birthday party, and track meet noted way beforehand.

    b. About two weeks ahead—that way, if an emergency comes up, you don't have to cancel a million things and disappoint anyone.

    c. Pretty much day by day.

Scoring

Review your answers, and total up how many of each letter you selected. Then, look up the letter that you chose most to see what your answers reveal about you!

Mostly A's: Your dependability vibe is **ULTRA GOOD**

When it comes to being responsible, you wrote the book. Your first thought in any and every situation is to do the right thing. All your friends know if there's anyone they can count on, it's you.

    Just be sure not to let people take advantage of your good nature. It's great that you're such a reliable gal, but don't forget to look out for *numero uno*—you! You don't have to make huge sacrifices to be a dependable friend. Continue to be responsible, but set boundaries that are within reason and take time to just chill.

Mostly B's: Your dependability vibe is **REAL DEAL IDEAL**

Congrats for understanding how to stay happy, healthy, and in control. You've achieved balance between being a good bud while not getting stepped on. That's great because it makes you a fairly dependable friend, yet you're not stressed out or overwhelmed by a sense of duty. You do things for the people who are important to you—like helping your BFF out with math—because you *want to*, not because you feel obligated.

    The prob? When you *do* set boundaries for yourself, you don't always know how to let people down gracefully. You might feel guilty when you have to tell a friend you can't lend a hand, so you make excuses rather than telling her straight. When you have to say "no" to a bud, be confident that it's the right decision for you and tell her honestly how you feel. ("I simply can't help you rearrange your room because I have too much homework this weekend.")

Mostly C's: Your dependability vibe is **A LITTLE FLIGHTY**

OK, you're not an airhead—let's get that straight right out of the gate. But, you might be a bit of a daydreamer. Or maybe you find the concept of continual responsibility boring. Or perhaps you genuinely forget to do things.

Sure, being dependable might not seem all that fresh and funky to you right now, but you can learn to like it! If someone is really asking you to take on a responsibility that you feel is invading your space, rather than blowing her off entirely, try to compromise: "I've got a load of homework to catch up on, so can I help you rearrange your bedroom next weekend instead? And then maybe you could help me clean *my* room."

Chapter 3

Boy, Oh, Boy!

Boys! They certainly aren't the be-all and end-all but, well, some of 'em sure are cute—and fun to crush on. Figure out where you fall in the crush department.

Who's Your Dream Dude?

When it comes to boys, there are loads of varieties out there to crush on. Do you go for radical skater dudes? Are brainiac boys more your speed? Or perhaps you're all starry-eyed over that cutie celeb? Whether you're boy-crazy or completely crush-free, this quiz will help you spy what kind of guy catches your eye.

1. You plan to spend Saturday night:

a. reading another book from the library's summer reading list.

b. watching baseball on TV with your dad.

c. at your BFF's sleepover, singing at the top of your lungs to every song on your favorite new CD.

d. baby-sitting. Once the kids are all tucked in, you'll take advantage of the solitude and chill in front of the tube.

e. at the movies. You and your BFF love catching a flick.

f. playing it by ear. You never make plans in advance. You like to keep your weekends spur-of-the-moment.

2. When your mom drops you off at the mall, you head straight to:

a. the book store. You might bump into some literary types.

b. the sporting goods department. The league's starting pitcher is often seen there, trying on the latest glove.

c. the CD store. Don't want to miss the newest cuties on the music scene.

d. the electronics department. It's packed with cool software and intensely introverted cyberhead sweeties.

e. the food court. You're meeting your friend Ethan for a smoothie and a smile.

f. wherever. No hot spots.

3. **If you wanted to let your crush know you like him, you'd:**

    a. E-mail or IM him some night, since he's always online.

    b. spend time at the go-cart track, where you know he'll be speed-racing with his pals.

    c. write an awesome fan letter to him. He's famous.

    d. copy a classic love poem and slip it in his mailbox.

    e. ask your bud Tim for advice—he knows how guys think.

    f. do nothing. When you don't know what to do, you don't do anything at all.

4. **If you were to receive a note signed, "Your Secret Admirer," you'd:**

    a. analyze the handwriting and try to uncover its sender.

    b. show it to your friends and encourage them to tell everyone at school—someone's bound to 'fess up.

    c. pretend it came from your favorite celeb.

    d. tell nobody, but be totally, privately thrilled.

    e. call your pal Sam to tell him his prank gave you a great laugh.

    f. tear it up and get on with your day.

5. **When you dream of you and your crush having a meal together, you picture:**

    a. sophisticated sushi for two.

    b. pizza and fries with the whole gang.

    c. whatever *he* likes. Make it something spicy!

    d. anything healthy, like a big salad.

    e. greasy onion rings with lots of ketchup, and your BFF.

    f. nothing. Hanging out with your crush? You'd rather hang with your buds.

6. **It's the first day of sleepover camp, and you walk into the dining hall with your new bunkmate. Which guy do you scope?**

    a. The boy who's won the talent show for the past three summers. Creative, artistic, smart—what more could you want?

b. The super-cool athlete whose amazing swimming skills make him king of the lake.

c. The new boy at the soda machine. He looks so much like a rock star.

d. The quiet guy staring at you over his grilled cheese. He has a great smile. Who knows?

e. Your best boy bud. You can't wait to see if he's taking water-skiing, too.

f. Forget the guys. You're too psyched to be with your summertime sisters to worry about a crush.

7. How would you spend a lazy afternoon?

a. Surfing the Net for some great back-to-school supplies. You always like to be prepared.

b. Hitting the mega-slide at the water park with your BFF.

c. Vegging in front of MTV. Musicians are so cute!

d. Mellowing in a yoga session with your mom.

e. Hangin' with your cousin Jake. You love beating him at video games.

f. Doing whatever comes your way.

8. The last thing you bought to give your wardrobe a jump and catch your crush's eye was:

a. a pair of super-chic super-smart green frames.

b. totally trendy plaid pants and a matching top.

c. a concert tee.

d. vintage Levi's.

e. new Nikes, just like your friend Justin wears.

f. who knows? Clothes are clothes.

9. Which of the following is easiest for you to memorize?

a. HTML code.

b. Names, positions, and stats of your favorite baseball players.

c. The birthdays of all the members of your favorite band.

d. Your fave Walt Whitman poem.

e. Your BFF Brian's phone number and e-mail address.

f. What was the question?

10. The celeb you most wish you could meet is:

a. Bill Gates, the founder of Microsoft.

b. The prez.

c. Justin Timberlake.

d. No one. You'd be too shy.

e. Matt Damon. He seems like he'd make such a nice older bro.

f. It'd be fun to meet a famous person but, if you never did, that would be OK.

11. You'd love to see your crush wearing:

a. a big backpack bulging with schoolbooks.

b. something from The Gap, of course.

c. the latest hip-hop look.

d. something casual and conservative, like khakis and loafers.

e. jeans and a tee.

f. whatever's comfortable.

12. What should a potential BF do to capture your heart?

a. Instigate a totally thought-provoking debate.

b. Know the full name of every kid at the YMCA.

c. Serenade you.

d. Be totally mellow.

e. BF? You're too busy hanging with your buds to get all mushy.

f. Just be himself.

Scoring

Give yourself:

6 points for each **a** answer.
5 points for each **b** answer.
4 points for each **c** answer.

3 points for each **d** answer.
2 points for each **e** answer.
1 point for each **f** answer.

Total up the points to find out what your crush vibe says about you.

12–19 Points: You like to GO WITH THE FLOW

You are totally laid-back about matters of the heart and life in general! You're always first in line to try new things, go to new places, and introduce yourself to new people. You would definitely give just about any guy a chance—even if he's your total opposite. This doesn't mean you'll hang out with just anyone—but you'd never pass up a chance to go see a Friday night movie just because your suitor is wearing the "wrong" shirt.

You don't have a "type" of guy you like—as long as he's being himself. You always have an open mind and a really positive outlook on things, and you're happiest just living life as it happens. Congrats on liking yourself first and foremost—and knowing that having a BF doesn't make you special. *You* make you special!

20–28 Points: You just think of guys as GOOD FRIENDS

Nothing wrong with that! By hanging with boys as friends, you'll get the inside scoop. Like what do they enjoy doing? Great! When you are ready to hang with a BF, you won't be intimidated by all the "guy stuff."

You might not be interested in having a BF just yet, and that's perfectly OK. It's awesome to have boys as buds. So, for now, just have tons of fun with your friends—guys *and* girls.

29–41 Points: You like SHY GUYS

Lots of guys are shy. But not all shy guys get to meet a great girl who'll see beyond the bashful smiles and blushing cheeks. You're clued in enough to know that still waters run deep. A strong, silent guy is often terrific BF material. He's not a showoff and tends to have interesting hobbies that take lots of quiet focus—like being a computer whiz.

When you do win him over and he starts talking, he probably has lots to express. If a shy guy smiles at you a lot, he probably likes you—at least as a potential bud. Break the ice by asking him a couple of questions so he knows you're interested in getting to know him better. You might be glad you did.

42–53 Points: You're a TRUE FAN

All your crush energy is focused on celebs—movie stars, TV studs, boy bands—you love 'em all. You tape all your favorite sitcoms, and you can't get enough MTV. Your walls are plastered with mega-talent. You keep up with Hollywood gossip and dream of a day when you might meet your celeb crush.

Enjoy your *fan*-tastic devotion, but keep your head out of the clouds. Keep in mind that celebrities are a fantasy.

54–63 Points: You go for BIG SHOTS

If a guy is popular and athletic, you're into him, no questions asked. Now, if he happens to be talented, sweet, generous, warm, and deserving of his rep, then terrific. But sometimes people who work really hard at being popular can be shallow—if popularity is all they care about. And just because he might hold the school record for the most soccer goals scored in one season, doesn't mean he's necessarily a great catch.

Want to test whether the supernova you're crushing on is worthy of your admiration? Check out how he treats other kids. Is he a jerk? Or, does he treat everybody well? Also, why is he popular? Has he worked super-hard during team practices? Is he funny? Or, does he simply hang with all the "right" people?

64–72 Points: You dig BRAINY BOYS

A guy's IQ is way more important to you than anything else. You like guys who have something intelligent to say. You love to learn and be challenged. You're probably pretty focused yourself. Or, maybe you like honor-roll hotties because you'd like to be more disciplined.

Often, we're attracted to people who have the qualities we wish for in ourselves. If your future BF is totally focused and ambitious, by all means share your hopes and dreams.

What's Your Sign?

ℋ♈♉♊♋♌♍♎♏♐
♎♏♐♑♒ℋ♈♉♊♋

Some say the signs of the zodiac have a major impact on your personality traits—and tell which boy could be your best match. See what stellar characteristics the stars point to in you, and discover your most compatible cosmic crush!

Aries the Ram
(March 21-April 19)

Ram, you are a leader, a forger, an innovator—even if you don't know it yet. With your headstrong personality and ambitious nature, you clear the path and pave the way for others to thrive in the wake of your success. But all in good time. Patience is not one of your stronger traits.

Cosmic Crush: A *Gemini* guy is pretty much your speed. He shares your live-life-to-the-fullest verve, which means he's fun—like you!

Taurus the Bull
(April 20-May 20)

Girl, you are one of the most loving, loyal, and dependable people around. Anybody who can call you a friend is lucky, indeed. And that's no bull. Wouldn't want to have a bud battle with you, though. You can be stubborn as a mule...er, bull.

Cosmic Crush: You could have lots in common with a *Libra* boy. You both appreciate nature's beauty. Hey, a hiking partner!

Gemini the Twins
(May 21-June 21)

If you're under the Twins sign, that means you're twice as fun! Your clever, quick-witted, and chatty ways make you the life of the party. But ignore that urge to be gossipy—it could mean double the trouble!

Cosmic Crush: You need a crush who can keep up with your gift for banter. An *Aquarius* boy should fit the bill.

Cancer the Crab
(June 22-July 22)

You have a heart of gold and a true knack for TLC. You know how to comfort and console with soul. You have the gift of empathy, and that's why others turn to you in times of

A Fun Way to Learn More About You

need. That is, if they can get your attention. You have a tendency to hide beneath your shell sometimes.

Cosmic Crush: Your idea of a great get-together with a boy is microwave popcorn and a DVD. A *Taurus* might be just your kind of guy.

Leo the Lion
(July 23-August 22)

Lioness, you are loyal, confident, and energetic. You seriously stand out from the rest of the pack—without even trying. Whether it's your flair for fashion or your magnetic smile, you're an attention nabber. Just don't let it get to your head. Self-centeredness is not attractive.

Cosmic Crush: Another *Leo* could be your perfect crush prospect. With twice the charisma, you two will be the most talked-about pair in school.

Virgo the Virgin
(August 23-September 22)

Perfectionism and attention to detail are your driving forces. This makes you a star student (teachers love your neatly organized notebooks) and impeccable dresser (you're perfectly accessorized at all times). But don't make yourself crazy trying to get everything *so* precise.

Cosmic Crush: Only another *Virgo* could possibly appreciate how hard you like to work. He'd probably make an excellent study buddy!

Libra the Balance
(September 23-October 23)

There's a whole lotta yakkety-yak going on in that noggin. You carefully think over *everything*—weighing the pros and cons, ups and downs, ins and outs. Once you voice your verdict, you do it with charm and grace—but sometimes with a dose of criticism. Careful.

Cosmic Crush: The fact that you find *Aries* guys irresistible can't be denied. That's because opposites attract, but you two could actually balance each other out.

Scorpio the Scorpion
(October 24-November 22)

Some might see you as reclusive, but you have a wild side. When you do something, you go all out! Your potential is limitless. Make careful choices so that your boundless energy never turns self-destructive.

Cosmic Crush: You could probably really connect with a *Pisces* boy on an emotional level—even if it's just as pals.

Sagittarius the Archer
(November 23-December 21)

You have a total sense of adventure, and you strive to thrive. Keep your eye on the target, and you should achieve everything you aim for. Prosperity just might be your middle name—but no looking down your nose at anybody now!

Cosmic Crush: A *Scorpio* boy is possibly your best bet in the crush department. He'll be able to keep up with your active spirit. In fact, he should find it challenging.

Capricorn the Goat
(December 22-January 20)

You get things done in a snap! That's because you're an expert at efficiency. You're sensible, reliable, patient, and responsible. If anybody can do the job (and do it well), it's you! You can be a little set in your ways, though, so loosen up a little.

Cosmic Crush: Smart girl, you take crushes lightly. A *Sagittarius* guy would be fun to hang out with—but nothing too serious!

Aquarius the Water Bearer
(January 21-February 18)

You don't like to follow the herd, but you love to be in the center of the crowd—even if it's chaotic. You like to be seen on the social scene, and your friendly, outgoing ways certainly make you stand out. Easy. It's one thing to shine—it's another to be over-the-top.

Cosmic Crush: A *Capricorn* can keep up with your quest to get to every main event. And when it comes time to tackle a community service project or something, you two work well together.

Pisces the Fish
(February 19-March 20)

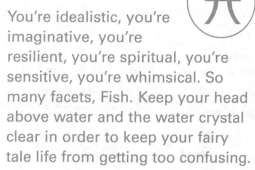

You're idealistic, you're imaginative, you're resilient, you're spiritual, you're sensitive, you're whimsical. So many facets, Fish. Keep your head above water and the water crystal clear in order to keep your fairy tale life from getting too confusing.

Cosmic Crush: You and a *Cancer* crush could have some deep-down conversations. It's cool to have a dude you can actually talk to.

A Fun Way to Learn More About You

What's Your Gabbing-With-Guys Groove?

No doubt there's pressure when it comes to chatting it up with boys. But how do you handle it? Do you get totally tongue-tied when talking to boys or, worse, do you turn mute? Identify your convo style, and then find out how to get the back-and-forth banter going with your crush!

1. This boy you've had your eye on for weeks is headed your way with a smile. You:

  a. calmly say, "Hey," and then move closer to start a convo.

  b. whisper, "What a cutie," to your friend.

  c. flash a smile and then panic.

  d. don't even notice him. You're late for practice.

2. You're chatting with your crush and there's a lull in the conversation. You:

  a. fire off a question. You've mentally filed some away just for moments like this.

  b. point out some people in the hall, and poke fun at them to start things up.

  c. cross your fingers that he'll say something.

  d. say, "Gotta go! See ya later!"

3. You've never talked to your crush on the phone, but his number is flashing on the Caller ID. You:

  a. grab the phone after the second ring. The moment you've been waiting for is here!

  b. answer it, hoping to keep your giggles under control.

  c. debate whether you should pick it up, because suddenly you're feeling dizzy.

d. pick up. You need to ask him something about your science homework.

4. You're on the phone with your BFF when she notices that your crush has just logged on. You:

a. thank your BFF, and then get online and say "hello" to him.

b. jump online and start IMing him—you're tons more comfy chatting with him this way.

c. sign on, just in case he sends you a message.

d. keep chatting with your BFF. You figure you'll catch him next time you're both online.

5. You're dying to know if your crush is going to the Valentine's Day dance with someone. You:

a. mention the dance in your next convo to see if he spills the beans.

b. convince your friend to ask him about it for you.

c. worry about it until you see him at the dance.

d. just ask him if he's going.

Scoring

Review your answers, and total up how many of each letter you selected. Then, look up the letter that you chose most and see what your answers reveal about you!

Mostly A's: GETTING TO KNOW YOU

As a get-to-know-you, chit-chat kind of gal, you've already figured out that your open, friendly attitude is important for smooth encounters with your crush. Talking to your crush is probably just as easy as talking to your BFF. Confidence = cool!

What's your next step? Make sure there are tons of opportunities for you two to keep getting to know each other better. Catch him in the hall, or at his locker for chats, and then invite him to hang out at the game with your friends. Just remember there's no need to rush a crush by being overly aggressive or declaring your feelings right away.

Mostly B's: GETTING THE GIGGLES

You're not all that shy, so why is it that you shy away from guys sometimes? Could it be your tendency to turn into a silly mess around your crush? We don't blame you for being psyched to talk to him and, yes, sometimes excitement can make you feel a little giddy and giggly. But, it's not fun—or positive—when a guy reduces you to a neurotic puddle.

If you haven't had a lot of crushes in your life, know that feeling comfortable (and staying cool) around boys *does* take time. Build up your conversation confidence by getting to know guys as friends first—even the ones you have crushes on. You'll feel more comfortable, which could help curb your giggle fit. If there is one particular boy who sends you into the giddy zone, try your best to remember that he's just a regular person who wants to know the real you—not Miss Gigglepuss.

Mostly C's: GETTING STAGE FRIGHT

Ever dash into the girls' bathroom to avoid running into your favorite cutie? We thought so. It's natural to sometimes panic when confronted with your crush, but in doing so you are also cutting off chances to make a real connection. You already know that you're a bright, fun girl who's full of opinions, interests and a dazzling sense of humor. Your crush needs to know that, too!

To get rid of some pressure so you can be yourself, keep a realistic outlook. Don't expect perfection every time you talk, because it's guaranteed there will be some quiet, awkward moments. They happen to everyone, but they don't have to feel weird. It's better to pause and think about what you're going to say than to blurt out the first thing that pops into your head. Start with group conversations before working up to one-on-one time with him. With the chat spread around to several people, you'll have more time to think—and more time to let him get to know you.

Mostly D's: GETTING TO THE POINT

Your no-nonsense, direct approach could be a big boost with your crush—you'll spend much less time having to hint or hide your feelings. The good news is you'll probably find out more quickly whether a crush is interested. The bad news is you may not be allowing either of you a fair chance, because relationships take time to build. It's great that you aren't into playing games, but don't forget that flirting can be fun. Chatting on the phone or online is how you start to build a relationship with someone—they get to know you, and you get to know them.

The next time you are tempted to cut a conversation short, why not just hang around for a few more minutes and ask him what he thought of the school play, or the basketball game on TV last night? Not only will that show him that you're interested in talking to him, it might give him a couple of extra minutes to work up the nerve to ask you what you're up to next weekend.

Can You Crack the Crush Code?

Now that you've got the conversation going with that boy, you hang on his every word and read his body language like a book. Or do you? Do you *really* know what he means when he says what he says and does what he does? He'd love it if you did. See how well you can read between the lines and decipher his hidden messages.

1. He waits for you after school so you can walk home together. It means:

a. that half-mile walk gives him fifteen full minutes every day to get to know you better.

b. he has no sense of direction and is still trying to learn the way home.

c. he's mighty fearful of stray dogs and wants protection.

2. He always tries to be your partner in science lab. It means:

a. he wants others to know there's a bit of *chemistry* between you.

b. he just happens to like that section of the room.

c. he wants to steal your hypothesis on algae growth.

3. He asks one of your friends what you're like—and *who* you like. It means:

a. he's really interested and is trying to send you a round-about message.

b. he really likes your friend and just needs an excuse to talk to her.

c. he's a gossip and plans to spread the word.

4. He's nice to you when you're alone, but distant and cold when he's with his friends. It means:

a. he really likes you, but his friends tease him mercilessly about his crushes.

b. he's two-faced and can't be trusted.

c. he has a multiple personality disorder.

5. He calls you up for no particular reason. It means:

　a. he's been thinking about you.

　b. he's just bored.

　c. he dialed the wrong number.

6. He tells you about his passion for bug collecting. It means:

　a. he's trying to open up to you.

　b. he loves the sound of his own voice.

　c. your backyard probably harbors a rare cicada species.

7. He tells you he's having trouble getting along with his math teacher and asks for your advice. It means:

　a. he respects your opinion.

　b. he's been asking for everybody's advice.

　c. he thinks you're the teacher's pet and can help him get on her good side.

8. You write him a soul-baring letter from camp—and he doesn't write back. It means:

　a. he's been spending time at his grandmom's and hasn't gotten your letter.

　b. your letter was a little overwhelming, and he needs some time to think about it.

　c. he gave you a fake address.

9. He teases you in front of your friends about your freckles. It means:

　a. he thinks your freckles are adorable.

　b. he also wants to tickle you when you least expect it.

　c. he's an insensitive creep.

10. You leave your jacket in the hall, and he shows up at your doorstep to give it back to you. It means:

　a. he is the kind of friend who will look out for you.

　b. he's hoping you'll invite him in for a snack.

　c. his mother made him do it.

11. He tells his friends you kissed him last week after school. But you didn't! It means:

a. he's a wishful thinker.

b. he's offering you a chance to test your powers of spin control.

c. he's trying to embarrass you.

12. You met at summer camp. He swore he'd never forget you. Now he's forgotten to respond to your phone message. It means:

a. he was amazed that you called, and he's trying to figure out how to respond.

b. he's decided he's not big on long-distance relationships.

c. he has amnesia.

13. He kindly offers to break the nose of the guy you're talking to during lunch. It means:

a. *he* wants to be the guy you're talking to during lunch.

b. he thinks the guy could benefit from a little rhinoplasty.

c. he forgot his lunch, and it's a lame attempt to steal the guy's sandwich.

14. He tells you he really likes you— really, *really* likes you. It means:

a. he really, *really* means it!

b. he's been reading on how to become a smooth-talker.

c. Mr. Sincere told your best friend the same thing yesterday!

Scoring
Give yourself:

3 points for each **a** answer.

2 points for each **b** answer.

1 point for each **c** answer.

Total up your points and read below to see how you did.

14–23 Points: You're a CLUELESS CODE-CRACKER

He might as well be talking to his goldfish for all the understanding he's getting from you right now. But, don't worry—you can still learn how to interpret his strange signs. If you're brave enough, find a quiet time to talk to him and ask for an explanation about the things that puzzle you.

24–33 Points: You're a MIXED-MESSAGES MANAGER

You're on the right track to getting at the real meaning of what he's saying and doing, but sometimes you get sidelined by his actions. Try to ignore the methods he uses to get his intentions across, and read between the lines a little bit. There *is* meaning to his sometimes seemingly nonsensical messages.

34–42 Points: You're a DUDE-TALK DICTIONARY

You're reading this guy like a book. You could probably get a part-time job as an emotional interpreter. You have a gift for finding the truth behind what a guy is trying to express—no matter how clumsy or awkward he is. This gift will serve you well throughout life. Learn to trust it, and keep developing it!

WHAT IN THE...?

OK, so you might or might not be picking up all his signals. But is it any wonder? When two people are getting to know each other, it's natural to be a little tongue-tied—especially when every word seems to be laden with importance and fraught with meaning. Take comfort in the fact that he's going through a lot of the same changes and insecurities as you. And, he's probably just as confused. Most likely, he's even less sure of how to proceed than you are.

It's hard for a guy to let his feelings be known when his crew is telling him that acting tough and aggressive is cooler than being expressive. Sometimes, he might not even know how he feels. Girls are often a lot more practiced at sharing and being in touch with their emotions. Topping it all off is the fact that girls are more mature than boys. It's quite possible that, even if a boy is absolutely gaga over you, he might not be ready to approach his feelings maturely. So, next time he teases you, it could just be his way of showing affection.

Are You Starstruck?

Have you ever had a crush on a movie star or celeb? Like, do you absolutely flip over boy bands, or drool over pictures of certain actors? There are different types of celebrity crushes, ranging from the "almost nonexistent" type, all the way to the "almost over the edge" type. To find out just how major or minor your crush is, clear your starry eyes long enough to take this quiz!

I. **You're talking on the phone to your best friend when you see your favorite celeb guy on a talk show. What do you do?**

 a. Politely wrap up your conversation so that you can go to the tube and hear what words of wisdom he has to say.

 b. Continue your conversation, sneaking a peek at the screen every now and then.

 c. Hang up on your best friend, sprint to the TV, and plant your lips on the screen.

2. **When you daydream about your star crush, what type of dream is it?**

 a. You imagine you have the chance to meet him in person and get his autograph.

b. You dream about how amazing he is, but that thought leads you to thinking about the cutie in your algebra class.

c. You fantasize about the day he'll propose to you. You'll marry right away, live in his two million-dollar mansion, and live happily ever after.

3. While reading a fan-zine, you come across an address where you can write to your star crush. How do you use that info?

a. Write a letter to him, stating that you are a fan and would like to request an autographed photo.

b. You don't. You're too busy to sit down and write fan mail to someone you'll probably never get an answer from anyway.

c. You write to your crush every week, pledging your undying love—and you make sure to include your phone number, asking him to call on a weekday, after seven, so you'll be home to answer the phone.

4. Your celebrity crush will be two hours from where you live, attending an awards show. What do you do?

a. You get there an hour early, hoping to snap a photo of him, and maybe get an autograph. You're there to have fun!

b. Nothing! Standing in a crowd of ten thousand screaming fans just to catch a glimpse of someone isn't your idea of a good time.

c. You arrive five hours early, wearing your best outfit, and waiting for your true love to pick you out of the crowd to join him.

5. You get the news that your star crush is dating a famous model named Zoë. How do you feel?

a. You're a little disappointed, but you want your celebrity hunk to be happy, so you wish him the best.

b. You've seen Zoë in fashion magazines. She's really beautiful, and they look like a great couple.

c. You are devastated! How could he do this to you? You find a picture of the famous model so that you can draw a mustache on her face. Then you go to the salon, get your hair done exactly like hers, and ask your friends to call you Zoë.

Mostly A's: MODERATELY STAR STRUCK

You sometimes have that famous guy on your mind a bit too often, but you keep the reality of the situation in check. Occasional daydreaming about your crush is harmless, as long as it doesn't interfere with your schoolwork or other important activities. You seem to see the big picture and realize that there are thousands of fans out there, just like you. You don't let your crush come between you and your everyday life, so it seems as though you can have your cake and eat it, too. You can keep your crush, but don't get too starry-eyed!

Mostly B's: YOUR STAR HASN'T STRUCK

You don't spend much time daydreaming about celebrities and fame. You're more into what's happening around you and have many outside interests. Sure, you can't help but admire some of those Hollywood hunks, but you'd rather focus your energy on getting that cute boy in your class to notice you.

Once in a while, writing a fan letter can be fun. Try writing to your favorite actor sometime—just for the heck of it. You never know, you might get a reply!

Mostly C's: STARSTRUCK TO INFINITY AND BEYOND

You've got it *bad* for your Hollywood heartthrob. You know almost every detail about him. He's on your mind much of the time, and you'd rather stay home and watch him on TV than go out with your friends.

You need to realize how many thousands of fans adore your crush, too. While you're waiting for the next-to-zero chance that you two might someday get together, you're letting your life pass you by. Your family, friends, and schoolwork must take precedence over him. Next time you have to choose between going out with friends or watching your crush on TV, try to compromise. Set your VCR to tape the program, go out with your friends, and save the video to watch on a rainy day. Why concentrate solely on a celebrity when that cute guy just winked at you from across the room?

Chapter 4

Cool with School

Aw, c'mon...it's not so bad, is it? School shapes you, enlightens you, gives you some *class*. Where would you be without an education? Here are a few quizzes you can take without the sweat of worrying about how your teacher will grade you. Give yourself some extra credit!

What Kind of Smart Are You?

Sure, maybe you score A's on all your tests in health class, or perhaps, at times you struggle to memorize dates for history. But do you really know how smart you are? Being smart is about a lot more than just a letter grade marked in red at the top of your book report. Besides reading and arithmetic, you can have A+ smarts in art, music, sports, nature, social situations, or in knowing yourself well. Most girls are actually a combination of a bunch of types of smart. Take this quiz to learn about your smart strengths. You can circle up to three choices for each question. Then, when you're finished, give yourself a gold star!

1. Your idea of a great weekend afternoon is:

a. curling up with a great new thriller in paperback.

b. rewriting the HTML code for your webpage.

c. sculpting a clay imitation of your crush.

d. going to an all-ages outdoor music festival with your buds.

e. competing in an in-line skating contest.

f. going down to the creek and scoring some new rocks for your collection.

g. going to a party at the new girl's house.

h. hanging out in your room and basking in the solitude.

2. When you go to a party, you tend to:

a. tell the amazing stories of your past summer camp experiences.

b. calculate how many pizzas should be ordered to ensure everybody gets at least two or three slices.

c. check out what everyone is wearing and what accessories work.

d. play the part of disc jockey.

e. dance the night away.

f. coax everybody outside for some impromptu stargazing.

g. make new friends.

h. relax on a folding chair and observe.

3. **The perfect gift for your b-day is a:**

   a. book club membership.

   b. laptop computer.

   c. painting easel and some pastels.

   d. CD.

   e. field hockey stick and some shin guards.

   f. year-long pass to a nearby state park.

   g. ticket to see a flick with six of your best friends.

   h. blank diary.

4. **When a new girl moves into the neighborhood, you know you're going to like her immediately if she:**

   a. says, "Read any good books lately?"

   b. challenges you to a game of chess.

   c. unveils a masterpiece she painted.

   d. plays bass.

   e. asks you to play some one-on-one basketball after school.

   f. invites you to join her on a day hike.

   g. invites you to her birthday party.

   h. doesn't pound on your door every thirty seconds.

5. **If you're meeting a friend at the mall and have some extra time to kill, you'd most likely spend it:**

   a. in the book store, perusing the fiction section.

   b. pricing software.

   c. comparing paint brushes in the art supply store.

   d. donning earphones at the record store.

   e. perfecting your putting skills at the sporting goods store.

   f. spending your allowance on a butterfly garden kit.

   g. looking for familiar faces in the food court.

   h. relaxing by the waterfall.

6. **You're in the candy store. You:**

   a. read the descriptions of each confection.

   b. figure out exactly how much you can afford.

c. check out the cool colors.

d. sing the songs from *Willy Wonka* to yourself.

e. open the bins and touch the candy.

f. check out all the different categories of candy.

g. chat with the lady who works behind the counter.

h. buy yourself whatever you want.

7. Your favorite school subject is:

a. English.

b. math.

c. art.

d. music.

e. phys ed.

f. science.

g. social studies.

h. study hall.

8. More than anything else, your ideal crush would have to appreciate:

a. the outstanding metaphors in the notes you pass to him during class.

b. that you might beat him at logic games.

c. having an occasional lunch in the sculpture garden outside the art museum.

d. Mozart.

e. ESPN.

f. long walks in the park.

g. hanging out with friends— yours.

h. that you two can share your innermost secrets with one another.

9. If you're working on a group project, you would prefer to:

a. do the book work and help write the text.

b. work out the math stuff.

c. make a cool poster to go with the presentation.

d. create a soundtrack.

e. act out the project as a skit.

f. research the scientific parts of the project.

g. be the presentation's main speaker.

h. work alone.

10. You're having a sleepover, and everyone decides to play a game. You'd vote to play:

a. Scrabble.

b. Monopoly.

c. Pictionary.

d. Name That Tune.

e. Twister.

f. Trivial Pursuit.

g. Family Feud.

h. Solitaire.

Mostly A's: WORD SMART
You're good at reading and writing, and also enjoy doing both just for fun. Plus, you're good at essay tests, crossword puzzles, storytelling, and word games. You learn best by saying, hearing, and seeing words.

Mostly B's: MATH SMART
You're like a human calculator. People who are math smart are good at solving brainteasers, playing logic and number games, or doing science experiments. You learn best by categorizing, solving problems, and classifying.

Mostly C's: PICTURE SMART
Do you see pictures when you close your eyes? People who are picture smart are talented artists and have a good eye for fashion. They also are great at jigsaw puzzles, mazes, and at reading maps. You learn best by drawing pictures or by using visual organizers.

Mostly D's: MUSIC SMART
Are you always humming tunes, singing, or tapping along to the beat? You might excel at playing an instrument or dream of being in a band. You learn best by putting ideas to music in your head or by listening to audio tapes that teach math, reading, or history.

Mostly E's: BODY SMART
Making the cut for varsity is a breeze. Dancers and actors are also body smart. Bottom line? You're good at using your hands or body for activities. You learn best by using hands-on materials or by acting out important ideas.

Mostly F's: NATURE SMART
You probably amaze people by the way you recognize plants, animals, or minerals. You enjoy experiencing and learning about nature. You learn best through classifying and sorting material into groups.

Mostly G's: PEOPLE SMART

People always comment on the fact that no matter where you go, you never quit smiling and saying "hello" to others. You have no trouble mixing with different groups and love to meet new people. You're probably involved in a lot of extracurricular activities and might be active in student government. You learn best by working with others.

Mostly H's: SELF SMART

You'd rather be far from the maddening crowds. You have no trouble hanging out with yourself. Maybe you like to write in a journal, pursue a hobby, or just think. You're the type of person who has no problem marching to the beat of a different drummer. You know yourself well, and sometimes others come to you with their problems. You learn best by working alone.

WHEN I GROW UP, I WANT TO...

Now that you know your intelligence strengths, check out some careers that could be perfect for a smart girl like you.

- **WORD SMART**: Librarian, writer, editor, journalist, TV announcer, lawyer, English teacher.

- **MATH SMART**: Accountant, mathematician, computer analyst, bookkeeper, pilot, doctor, scientist, astronaut.

- **PICTURE SMART**: Architect, graphic artist, interior decorator, photographer, artist, fashion editor, chef, sculptor.

- **MUSIC SMART**: Disc jockey, musician, music therapist, songwriter, studio engineer, choral director, conductor, singer, music teacher.

- **BODY SMART**: Physical therapist, recreational worker, dancer, actor, mechanic, carpenter, physical education teacher, choreographer, professional athlete, jeweler.

- **NATURE SMART**: Naturalist, park ranger, botanist, marine biologist, zoologist, forest ranger, entomologist, wildlife photographer.

- **PEOPLE SMART**: Manager, school principal, sociologist, counselor, clergy woman, public relations executive, politician, salesperson, entrepreneur, social director.

- **SELF SMART**: Psychologist, detective, spy, counselor, headhunter, agent, therapist.

Do You Know How to Analyze Your Handwriting?

The way you cross your t's and dot your i's supposedly says a lot about your personality. To analyze your handwriting, break out the book report you wrote last night. Or, copy some text out of this book! Then check below to see what your handwriting style reveals about you.

Slant of individual letters

Letters slant to the right
When letters tilt strongly to the right, it means you have an impatient streak. You prefer to make up your own rules instead of following orders from other people. You probably speak quickly, so people need to listen carefully if they want to keep up with you!

The man went to the store to

Letters have little or no slant
When letters don't tilt strongly to the left or right, it means you have an easygoing personality. Your theme is "Go with the flow." You're equally as comfortable doing your own thing as working within a group. You're very reliable. You're also good at keeping promises and sticking to a schedule.

The man went to the store to

Letters slant to the left
When letters tilt to the left, it means you have a strong sensitive side. You are highly in tune with the energy of people around you, and negative environments really bring you down. Try to laugh more and to not take criticism so personally. Work on growing a thicker skin!

The man went to the store to

Shape of individual letters

Lots of loops, circles, and curves

If you're a little "loopy," it means you have a dramatic and artistic personality. You like to do things that will get you noticed. Your dress and hairstyle might be larger than life, and you love being the center of attention. You are a natural performer, so music and the arts might be attractive to you.

The man went to the store to

Up and down lines, and jagged corners

If your writing has lots of sharp lines and points, it means you'd rather be by yourself than with others. You are a very private person who needs to be alone in order to recharge your batteries. You are easily stressed out by noise and by loud people. You need a sanctuary where you can play music or work on projects that lift your spirits.

The man went to the store to

Mixture of cursive and printing styles

Writing that includes a mixture of cursive and printing styles means that you are indecisive. One minute you're up, the next you're down. Today you're in love, tomorrow you can't stand your former sweetie. It's important for you to find some middle ground, because you are always going to extremes. Balance is key!

The man went to the store to

Thickness of writing

Very thick and heavy

If you write using a lot of pressure and make thick lines, it means you have extra confidence. You know that what you have to offer is worthwhile, and you aren't afraid to speak up. Others might, at times, find you intimidating, but it's important for you to always express your opinion! You may need to learn how to listen to people, because you tend to hog the spotlight.

The man went to the store to

Medium thickness

If you write with a medium thickness, it means you have a "take it or leave it" attitude. You rarely overreact because you're in control of your emotions. You don't hold grudges, and you have a positive approach to relationships. You trust others easily and are quick to make new friends.

The man went to the store to

Very thin and spidery writing

Thin writing using light pressure means that you are a dreamer. You have trouble anchoring yourself in this world because you are always playing out scenes in your head. With your strong imagination, you could make an excellent writer or artist. And, playing sports or working out will keep you more grounded.

The man went to the store to

Direction of slope in sentences

Text slopes upward at the end of a sentence

If your sentences tend to slope upward, it means you have a need to please. You will go that extra mile in order to win somebody's approval. You know how to work a crowd and gain popularity through hard work. You're a natural politician, whether you realize it or not!

The man went to the store to

Text looks even and balanced at the end of a sentence

If your sentences don't slope up or down but stay somewhere in the middle, it means you are an excellent communicator. You work well in groups and enjoy team sports or acting in plays. You need energy from other people to keep you going, and you don't do as well when you're left alone.

The man went to the store to

Text slopes downward at the end of a sentence

If your sentences slope downward, it means you have a unique outlook on life. You are creative and inventive, and other people might not always understand where you are coming from. Sometimes you might feel like an "alien" because you view the world very differently from others. Stick to your guns—your special talents will be noticed one day!

The man went to the store to

Are You Fit for Gym Survival?

Are you one of those work-hard, play-hard athletes who lives for competition? If you answered, "Yes!" stop reading right now. You probably love gym class. But for the less athletically inclined who might have answered this question otherwise, gym class can be frightful. Take this quiz to find out where you fall on the workout tolerance scale. Don't worry—no matter where you rank, the gym advice in the scoring section should vastly improve your skills. So get ready, get set...go!

1. It's time to change clothes, and you're embarrassed about everyone seeing you practically naked. You plan to:

a. sneak into a nearby bathroom stall, and change your clothes like Clark Kent changed into Superman.

b. dress quickly and quietly, realizing everyone's too busy to notice you.

c. hire a large marching band to cause a distraction far away from your locker.

2. Your gym outfit makes you look like a string bean in a pillowcase. You decide to:

a. deal with it. It's an hour of your life.

b. accessorize. A belt and earrings can add magic to any outfit.

c. make a pup tent with the shorts, set up camp, and refuse to come out.

3. The gym teacher announces today's game is field hockey and asks you to line up for picking teams. You think:

a. "Maybe if I hold my breath, I can make myself pass out."

b. "I promise that somehow, someday, I will change the system."

c. "Field hockey? What's field hockey?"

4. During a game of dodgeball, the ball comes flying toward you at Lear-jet speed. Your plan is to:

a. scream, "Incoming!" and duck if decapitation looks likely.

b. run up to the ball, catch it, and send it hightailin' back to the other side.

c. contemplate how you'll look with a nose cast.

5. It's your turn to climb the ceiling-high rope for physical fitness day. You will:

a. go hand over hand as high as you can.

b. announce you're allergic to rope fiber, and, must sadly, sit this one out.

c. get a good running start, grab the rope, and try to swing like Tarzan through a nearby escape window.

6. You're running around playing soccer in the sun when you start feeling kind of woozy and sick. You:

a. play 'til you drop. You'll be OK, and the team needs you.

b. realize that the girl who volunteered to be goalie might be smarter than you thought.

c. tell the teacher, get some water, and sit out for a while.

7. You're at bat. Bases are loaded, and the winning run is on third—ready to slide in to home. Your strategy is to:

a. swing at everything, including bees and other bugs.

b. concentrate on making contact with the ball.

c. bring the teacher to tears with the stirring, "If you build it, they will come..." scene from *Field of Dreams*. As he sobs, you take your base.

8. The boys have been brought in to your gym class for square dancing, and you've been paired with the King of the Dorks. You:

a. get through it as best you can. It probably won't be that bad.

b. call MTV to find out how you can dance in a music video.

c. fling yourself into a nearby wall and knock yourself unconscious when he swings you 'round.

Scoring

Yep, this one has correct answers. Here's a breakdown:

1. **b:** You can bet that everyone in the locker room is just as concerned about being seen *el starko* as you are. So remind yourself that no one is really looking at you, and change your clothes. If possible, avoid heading to the bathroom, which just draws more attention. And, hiring a marching band is a clever idea, but simply too expensive.

2. **a:** Everyone feels silly wearing gym outfits, and the slickest accessories in the world couldn't make them attractive (we've tried—oh, how we've tried). This is gym, not a fashion show. The shorts are made to be practical for jumping, bending, and running. One hint: You know the Lycra-wear that basketball players don under their baggy shorts? It can save you from a lifetime of "I see London, I see France...."

3. **b:** For non-athletes, waiting to be picked for teams is often excruciating. One thing you can do is talk to your gym teacher after class, and ask if she'd please handle dividing people into teams. Explain how much better gym class would be without that added pressure. She'll probably understand, and you might even become the class hero. If not, continue to forgo hyperventilating. It's much easier to run when you can breathe.

4. **a and b:** If you're terrified of high-speed balls, it's time to face your fear. With a sibling or friend, practice playing catch in the backyard. It could take a few sessions, but you'll eventually get the hang of it. Still, if the class terror whips the ball at your head, duck. Safety first.

5. **a:** Step one is to seize the rope and climb with everything you've got. Then, push yourself a little farther. Once you feel shaky, carefully lower yourself down the rope—do not slide down. Painful! Step two is to do something about those muscles. A set of ten push-ups every other night might do the trick. Ask your gym teacher for suggestions on how to get stronger. She'll be impressed, and you'll get some form.

6. **c:** Tell your teacher you're feeling sick, and then go sit in the shade. And, ask someone to get you some water. Next time, drink plenty of liquids *before* gym class if you know you'll be playing soccer in what feels like the Sahara.

7. **b:** First of all, be realistic. You can't possibly be responsible for the team losing. If you strike out, that's *one* out. There were two others before you.

So, focus on the ball and watch your bat make contact. Keep your bat level, and swing through. Then drop it and run like the wind. If you *do* strike out, don't give up faith. Ask your team's batting pro for some pointers, and have a friend or family member practice hitting and pitching with you at home.

8. **a:** Square dancing is a fun gym class activity for about two kids. Still, there's no reason to make a scene just because your partner is not super slick. Everyone's just trying to get through it, and so should you. Besides, your dorky partner might know how to do-si-do like nobody's business!

What's Your Class Clown Status?

We all envy the girls who can make a whole crowd burst into instantaneous laughter. We've seen what the hilarious can do, from lifting burdens and easing awkward silences to making the most stone-faced teachers giggle by turning lunch into a side show. But, while only a lucky few are natural-born comedians, almost *anyone* can develop a great sense of humor. If you want to see where you fall on the good humor scale, take the challenge below. And then check out the no-fail hints on how to pack your jokes with punch.

I. When you say to a friend, "Have you heard the one about…":

  a. she rolls her eyes, exclaiming, "About a bazillion times."

  b. she smiles, encouraging you to continue.

  c. she says she hears her gold-fish calling.

2. When telling the punch line of a joke, you're likely to:

  a. flub all the words because you get so darn excited.

  b. make it somewhere between twenty minutes too short and two hours too long.

  c. crack yourself up so much that you can't get the words out.

d. make sure you have the crowd's attention—then wow 'em.

3. A typical response to your joke-telling is:

a. "And the punch line was *what*?"

b. "Man, I've got to write that one down!"

c. "Sorry, did you say something?"

4. Which of the following strikes you as funny?

a. Knock-knock jokes.

b. Pretty much every episode of *Friends*.

c. None of the above.

5. Nothing makes you laugh quite like:

a. that kid who does total improv in the cafeteria every day.

b. a pop quiz—you always get a case of nervous giggles.

c. the comics section of the Sunday newspaper.

6. During recess, you get beaned in the head with a kickball. You're not hurt, but you feel like a total dufus. Your new crush is now hovering over you, asking if you're OK, so you respond:

a. "No! Can't you see I'm hurt?"

b. "Yes, but next time I'm wearing my kickball helmet."

c. "Grandma? Is that you?"

7. The definition of "spoof" is:

a. that annoying tuft of hair that won't stay down.

b. a humorous imitation of something.

c. the crusty gunk that sticks to the bottom of pots and pans.

d. a comedian who does impersonations of famous celebs.

8. Which of the following would you be willing to do for a laugh?

a. Stick peas in your nose, and shoot them out on command.

b. Spin yourself silly, and walk through a crowded airport.

c. Wear a dress and snowshoes to school—with no explanation.

d. Belt out show tunes over the school intercom.

e. None of the above.

9. You can remember a funny joke for approximately:

a. a lifetime—and beyond, if it's good enough.

b. a month or so.

c. the time it takes you to walk away from the person who told it.

10. You hold up a funky pair of sandals and ask your bud what she thinks of them. Determine which statements are puns and which are sarcasm.

a. "I love them. They'll be a shoe-in at the party!"

b. "Do they come with oars?"

c. "I think they'll look fantastic—in a box under your bed."

d. "Cool shoes—they have a lot of sole."

11. When telling a joke, it's really important that you:

a. speak clearly.

b. wear trendy clothes.

c. announce, "This is the best joke ever!"

d. keep your eyes on the ground.

12. What is the best response you can get after telling a joke?

a. A titter.

b. A snicker.

c. A guffaw.

d. A smirk.

Scoring
Award yourself the proper amount of points for each answer. Tally them up, and check your analysis on the next page.

1. a. 1 **b.** 3 **c.** 1

2. a. 1 **b.** 1 **c.** 2 **d.** 3

3. a. 1 **b.** 3 **c.** 1

4. a. 2 **b.** 3 **c.** 1

5. a. 3 **b.** 1 **c.** 3

6. a. 1 **b.** 2 **c.** 3

7. a. 1 **b.** 3 **c.** 1 **d.** 2

8. a. 2 **b.** 3 **c.** 3 **d.** 3 **e.** 1

9. a. 3 **b.** 2 **c.** 1

10. (give yourself 3 points for each correct answer)
a. pun **b.** sarcasm **c.** sarcasm **d.** pun

11. a. 3 **b.** 1 **c.** 2 **d.** 1

12. a. 2 **b.** 1 **c.** 3 **d.** 1

11–23 Points: You're a TOO-SERIOUS SISTER

Often, everyone around you is cracking up, but you just don't get it. Maybe you're having trouble making connections (in which case it's time to clue in and pay attention), or maybe you come from a family that's not too keen on laughter. Try stepping into the sillier side of life once in a while. If you're having a tough time chuckling, go for an outside source. Rent a funny movie, read a humorous book, scan the Internet for silly "Top 10" lists, or call a friend who makes you laugh. Go ahead—a few rounds of guffaws will do your body good.

24–35 Points: You're a HAM-IN-TRAINING HOPEFUL

OK, so you're not exactly Jim Carrey—or Drew Carey, for that matter. Still, you've been known to deliver a good joke or two—and even pull off a successful prank. While you sometimes wish you could think of quicker comebacks or wittier comments, you still manage to see the humor in everyday life.

36–48 Points: You're a JOKE-JAMMIN' JESTER

Ha-ha! You have that special way of making people giggle before you even start telling a joke. You're used to being in the limelight and feel right at home wisecracking to a crowd. You have an ability that others only dream of possessing. And best of all, unlike good looks, you will be able to bank on this gift for the rest of your life. Keep spreading the guffaws!

PERFECT YOUR DELIVERY

Ways to make your jokes strike it big

1. **SPEAK CLEARLY.** Even the funniest joke will stink if no one can understand you.

2. **DON'T RUSH.** Develop a moment of suspense before saying the punch line. Allow your joke to unfold—it's like telling a good story.

3. **CUT TO THE CHASE.** While you don't want to rush the joke, you don't want to lose your audience by dragging the story on too long either. Keep up a nice lively pace.

4. **MAINTAIN EYE CONTACT.** A joke doesn't pack the same wallop if you stare at your shoes. Look into the listener's eyes.

5. **KEEP IT EXCITING.** Keep your voice upbeat and excited. Make gestures with your hands and face to help express yourself energetically.

6. **KEEP IT CLEAN.** If a joke might be even a teeny-weeny bit offensive, don't tell it.

7. **DON'T CRACK YOURSELF UP.** Nothing's more annoying than someone who laughs too hard to get the punch line out.

8. **REHEARSE YOUR JOKE.** Telling a good joke takes practice, so tell it to a mirror before going live.

9. **SAVE FACE IF IT BOMBS.** If your joke falls flat, try sarcasm: "Tough crowd, eh?"

10. **DON'T GIVE UP.** Even star comedians bomb now and then. It'll get better.

Do You Have the "Write" Stuff?

Even if your English teacher doesn't require it, keeping a journal is a great way to learn more about yourself. It can be a place to record daily happenings or serve as an outlet for emotions, poetry, lists, quotes, artwork...anything. Your journal can be a fancy leather diary or a plain spiral notebook. Write every day, on special occasions, or when the mood hits. Keep your work private, or share it with others. Every journal (and journal keeper!) is unique. Here are five journaling activities to get you started.

1 **Write about your personal philosophy.**
Don't have one? Well, it's time to get one. Ponder some of life's questions: "Who am I? Why is my life meaningful? What are my goals, and how can I achieve them?" You don't have to know the answers. The point is to think deeply about each question, and open yourself up to new possibilities. Don't censor what you write—just let the words flow naturally.

2 **Keep a dream journal.**
Dream journals are useful windows into the subconscious. Each night when you sleep, your brain creates wonderful adventures that help you work through your problems. Dreams often contain rich symbolism, and a dream journal helps tap into a dream's hidden meaning. Place your journal beside your bed with a pen. Before you sleep, repeat in your head, "I will remember my dreams." As soon as you wake, try to recall your dreams. Don't be discouraged if you can't remember them at first. They'll get easier to recall. Even if you only remember fragments, write them down. Your dreams might become more vivid as you write. Don't worry about grammar or spelling. And consider consulting a dream dictionary. It can help decipher the messages in your dreams.

3 **Write a letter... to yourself!**
Once a year, write yourself a letter. Reflect on the past year, state your goals for the upcoming year, and remind yourself of what

you want from life. The next year, read your letter and write a new one for the upcoming year.

4 Start a travel log.
If you enjoy traveling—even if you've never left your home state—a travel log is great for recording your thoughts and feelings about new places. Take your log with you on vacation to pass time while in the car or on the plane. Rarely travel? Use your log to write about a cool restaurant or bookstore in your area.

5 Make a collage journal.
By cutting pictures from magazines, newspapers, and postcards (or drawing them yourself), you can create a journal of your hopes, goals, and fears. Use artwork and poetry to make a collage of who you are now, how you think others see you, or who you want to be a year from now. If one goal is to get in shape, cut a picture of a fit body from a magazine, attach it to your journal, and paste your head onto the body. Want to be more friendly? Draw a picture of yourself with a big smile surrounded by lots of things you love. Add your favorite inspirational quotes or jokes. When you feel unexcited about life, look at your collages for motivation.

The Popularity Myth

Chapter 5

True or false? Being on the "it" list is where it's at! Guess what...that's total fiction. Here's the truth: Popularity isn't about being in one particular group or wearing the "right" clothes. Anybody can be popular—well-known and well-liked. No matter whom you hang with, you are going to be perceived by other people in a certain way. It's up to you to let your truest self shine through.

How Far Would You Go to Be Popular?

It seems like every kid on the planet wants to be that word that starts with P. But would you sacrifice your own true self to clamber your way up the social ladder? How important is "popularity" to you, really? Some girls are willing to do just about anything to be part of the "in" crowd...an A-lister... at the top of the social scene. Are you one of them?

1. You are talking to some of the most popular girls in school when they start saying mean things about one of your friends. You:

a. stick up for your friend. Who cares about being popular?

b. walk away. You won't diss your friend, but you can't help it if the popular girls do.

c. laugh along with them. Sure, your friend is nice, but she isn't going to get you in with the cool girls.

2. You and your mom have planned a mother/daughter day. She's been talking non-stop about it for weeks. You've never seen her so excited. Then, a popular girl calls you and asks you if you want to go to a movie with her the same day. You say:

a. "Sure, I have nothing else to do anyway." Then you ask your mom to drive you to the theater.

b. "Gee, normally, I would love to go—but, today, I already have plans with my mom."

c. "I really want to, but I am going out with some other friends today." You're not going to tell her you're going out with your mom!

3. You are at the mall with some popular kids. While in a jewelry store, one of them steals an expensive pair of earrings. You:

a. ask her to put them back, but make sure she knows you are not going to rat her out.

b. don't say anything about it. Anyway, it's the security staff's fault for not paying closer attention.

c. yell at her in front of everyone, making such a commotion that the store manager comes to see what's going on.

4. Your dad has made you swear not to touch his beloved new computer. When a cool girl is at your house and asks to use it, you say:

a. "No way! My dad would ground me for life if I touched it." And that is the truth.

b. "Oh, I'm so sorry, but it broke this morning. How about watching a movie instead?"

c. "Oh, sure. Do whatever you want." You secretly hope your dad will never find out.

5. A popular girl, who would never normally talk to you, comes up to you right before a math quiz and asks you to help her cheat. You:

a. tell her you would, but that you didn't study, either. Telling one measly little lie is better than cheating, right?

b. yell, "Um, I missed the *American Music Awards* to study for this quiz. I don't think I am going to help you cheat."

c. tell her she can cheat off you anytime. After all, she *is* popular.

6. At your best bud's birthday party, a popular girl asks you to blow off the party and go hang out somewhere else. You say:

a. "I would love to, but it's my best bud's party. Why don't you stay? It'll be fun."

b. "Sure. This party is a drag."

c. "Why would I? It is my best bud's party. It would be rude to leave."

7. You pride yourself on never lending out money. A cool girl comes up to you and asks to borrow $20. You say:

a. "Of course. Here, take $40."

b. "Oh, I'm sorry. I only have $5," even though your wallet is full of money.

c. "Oh, I can't. You see, I never lend money to anyone."

Scoring

Add up your points, and read on to see what your answers say about you.

1. a. 3	b. 2	c. 1	**5.** a. 2	b. 3	c. 1
2. a. 1	b. 3	c. 2	**6.** a. 2	b. 1	c. 3
3. a. 2	b. 1	c. 3	**7.** a. 1	b. 2	c. 3
4. a. 3	b. 2	c. 1			

7–11 Points: You find POPULARITY TOO IMPORTANT

Well, let's just say, you need to learn that being popular isn't such a big deal. You seem to drop everyone and everything that's important to you when a popular person gives you any iota of attention. Hold on to your real friends— the ones who don't expect you to compromise your convictions.

12–16 Points: You're in the middle of the POPULARITY POLE

You want to be popular, but you'd never stomp on anyone on your way up the social ladder. You understand the importance of friends and family. On the other hand, you're still willing to tell little fibs to avoid looking like a dork in front of the popular people. Be careful.

17–21 Points: You have POPULARITY IN PERSPECTIVE

You go, girl! You don't let anyone come between you and your morals. Your loyal personality will gain trust and respect from people who deserve it. You understand that, in the grand scheme of things, popularity is not the most important thing in the world.

How Do Others See You?

Everybody can see that you have your hair pulled up in a ponytail and you're wearing a green sweater. But do you want to get the scoop on how others perceive you? Answer ten simple questions to find out if you're considered to be a wallflower, a wild child, or somewhere in between!

1. When do you feel your best?

  a. In the morning.

  b. During the afternoon and early evening.

  c. Late at night.

2. You usually walk:

  a. fairly fast, taking long steps.

  b. fairly fast, taking short, quick steps.

  c. moderately, with your head up, looking the world in the face.

  d. slow, with your head down.

  e. very slow.

3. When talking to people, you:

  a. stand with your arms folded.

  b. have your hands clasped.

  c. have one or both of your hands on your hips.

  d. gently touch or tap the person to whom you are talking.

  e. play with your ear, touch your chin, or smooth your hair.

4. When relaxing, you sit with:

  a. your knees bent, and your legs neatly side by side.

  b. your legs crossed.

  c. your legs stretched out or straight.

  d. one leg curled under you.

5. When something really amuses you, you react with:

a. a big, appreciative laugh.

b. a laugh, but not a loud one.

c. a quiet chuckle.

d. a sheepish smile.

d. Green.

e. Dark blue or purple.

f. White.

g. Brown or gray.

6. **When you go to a party or social gathering, you:**

a. make a loud entrance so everyone notices you.

b. make a quiet entrance, looking around for someone you know.

c. make an almost silent entrance, trying to stay unnoticed.

7. **You're working and concentrating very hard, when you're interrupted. Do you:**

a. welcome the break?

b. feel extremely irritated?

c. vary between these two extremes?

8. **Which of the following colors do you like most?**

a. Red or orange.

b. Black.

c. Yellow or light blue.

9. **When you are in bed at night, in the last few moments before falling asleep, you lie:**

a. stretched out on your back.

b. stretched out, face down on your stomach.

c. on your side, slightly curled.

d. with your head resting on one arm.

e. with your head under the covers.

10. **You often dream that you are:**

a. falling.

b. fighting or struggling.

c. searching for something or someone.

d. flying or floating.

e. doing nothing. You usually have a dreamless sleep.

f. happy.

Scoring

Add up your points, and read below to see what your answers say about you.

1. **a.** 2 **b.** 4 **c.** 6

2. **a.** 6 **b.** 4 **c.** 7 **d.** 2 **e.** 1

3. **a.** 3 **b.** 2 **c.** 5 **d.** 7 **e.** 6

4. **a.** 4 **b.** 6 **c.** 2 **d.** 1

5. **a.** 6 **b.** 4 **c.** 3 **d.** 2

6. **a.** 6 **b.** 4 **c.** 2

7. **a.** 6 **b.** 2 **c.** 4

8. **a.** 6 **b.** 7 **c.** 5 **d.** 4 **e.** 3 **f.** 2 **g.** 1

9. **a.** 7 **b.** 6 **c.** 4 **d.** 2 **e.** 1

10. **a.** 4 **b.** 2 **c.** 3 **d.** 5 **e.** 6 **f.** 1

Less Than 21 Points: Others see you as NERVOUS NELLY

People think you are shy, nervous, and indecisive—someone who needs looking after, who always wants others to make her decisions. They see you as a worrier who always conjures up problems that don't exist. Only those who know you well know the real you.

21–30 Points: Others see you as CAREFUL KELLY

Others see you as very cautious and careful. It'd really surprise them if you ever did something impulsive or on the spur of the moment—they're expecting you to examine everything carefully from every angle, and then usually decide against it. They think this reaction is caused partly by your prudent nature.

31–40 Points: Others see you as VERY SHY VAL

Others see you as sensible, cautious, careful, and practical. They see you as clever, gifted, or talented—but still modest. Not a person who makes friends too quickly or easily, but someone who's extremely loyal to friends she does make, and who expects the same loyalty in return. Those who really get to know you realize it takes a lot to shake your trust in friendships, but also that it takes you a long time to get over it, if that trust is ever broken.

41–50 Points: Others see you as a NICE-AS-PIE PAL

Others see you as fresh, lively, charming, amusing, practical, and always interesting. Someone who's constantly the center of attention, but well-balanced enough to not let it go to her head. You're also seen as kind, considerate, and understanding. Someone who'll always cheer others up and help them out.

51–60 Points: Others see you as a GET-UP-AND-GO GAL

People see you as exciting and having a rather impulsive personality. You're a natural leader and quick to make decisions. Others see you as bold and adventuresome—someone who will take chances. They enjoy being in your company because of the excitement you radiate.

More Than 60 Points: Others see you as SELF-ASSURED SALLY

Some see you as a person they should handle with care because you could have a tendency to dominate. Others might admire you, wishing they could be more like you—very self-assured.

What's Your Favorite Color?

When you shop for clothes, what color are you instantly drawn to? And which shade do you like to use when you are decorating your walls? Your favorite color reveals a lot about your personality. Read below to find out what your fave shade says about the real you.

Red

You drama queen, you! If you love red, it means that you are outgoing and love being the center of attention. One thing that you may need to watch, though, is that hot temper of yours. Because you are strong-willed, it can be easy to get into shouting matches with people about silly things. You may need to learn how to count to ten before you speak—or maybe even eleven or twelve!

Orange

You're a real bud! If you favor orange, you're a happy person with a positive attitude about life. When people meet you, they know right away that they've found a friend. Your gentle spirit and sweet energy may attract "strays"—not just the fuzzy animal kind, but people who are down on their luck or have been rejected by the "cool" crowd. And, your sympathetic ear makes people feel comfortable confessing their innermost secrets to you.

Yellow

You love clowning around! If yellow is your favorite color, you've probably been voted the "Funniest Kid in Class" at least once. You have a great sense of humor and are known to act goofy, especially when you're trying to cheer somebody up. You could easily turn your talent for performing into a hobby, or even a career. Try auditioning for the school play or singing in a musical group. Bet you'll be signing autographs before you know it!

A Fun Way to Learn More About You

Green

If you love green, you are a natural psychologist. You have an eerie knack for sizing up someone the minute you meet him or her. But people might find your smarts a bit intense. Because you can figure things out pretty quickly, you tackle problems both at school and in your personal life without blinking an eye. Your sense of poise and calm allow you to succeed in almost any situation.

Blue

If you are drawn to blue, you are emotional and big-hearted. Sometimes you can get so caught up in what other people are feeling that you ride their ups and downs with them. You have times when you're very sensitive—crying one minute and laughing the next. You need to stay grounded with physical activities like sports or working out. Sweating it out can help balance your emotions if you're getting too extreme.

Pink

Creativity is your middle name! If pink intrigues you, you are totally imaginative. You're the one who always comes up with that extra special way of doing things. You love color, arts and crafts, and even computer graphic design. In school, you might be ahead of your time, but keep developing those talents. After graduation, you could rise to the top in any field where creativity counts.

Gray

Stand up and be counted! If gray is your best shade, you'd rather work behind the scenes and pretend that you're invisible. When people are focused on you, your shyness can make you nervous. You're really good at sharing credit with others and helping friends pursue their dreams. You just need to learn how to be bolder and seize the spotlight for yourself once in a while. And, learn to speak up!

Brown

You've never met an animal that you didn't like. If you love brown, you feel very connected to nature and love critters of every kind. You're most at home outdoors, and you love hiking, biking, or water sports. Crowded places and cities are not your thing. You could be a great park ranger, zoo-keeper, or even a veterinarian. Whatever your choices might be, your giftedness with plants and animals will be with you through-out your life.

Beige

Can we say, "mellow"? If you're drawn to shades of tan and beige, you have the ability to blend in with any crowd. You have friends from different social scenes and get along with almost anybody. You'd be a good politician, with your talent for chatting people up—or a great marketing or salesperson. At school, you could be voted class president or head of your favorite club. Working at a store could also be fun, because you like people.

Purple

"No autographs, please." If you love the color purple, you have a special magnetism that draws all eyes your way. You are powerful and larger than life, and people find you attractive. You could use this energy to become a model or performer, and boys hover around you like bees. Your challenge may be to learn how to work hard, because sometimes things get handed to you. You're not *always* going to be the teacher's pet!

Black

If you love black, you love being mysterious and don't like other people knowing your business. You may have unusual hobbies or style, and sometimes people might hassle you because your tastes are different from theirs. But don't let the frustration get to you. Some people are threatened by those who have their own vision. Stand your ground, and dare to be unique!

White

"Don't sweat it," is your motto. If white is your color, you are a very balanced person. People might call you an open book because you seem to have nothing to hide. You live life simply and avoid complicated relationships or unpleasant social groups. Your no-nonsense approach to life leaves you with plenty of energy to focus on the important things. Your taste for charity work and your appreciation of the environment will help you to make a real difference!

Is Your Style Totally Unique?

Yeah, you're stylin'. You spend every evening picking out the perfect outfit to wear the next day. You wouldn't be caught dead in the wrong threads. But do you put the "you" in unique? Find out if you are a fad follower, an "I couldn't care less what people think of my style" gal, or if you are on middle ground (when it comes to your clothes anyway).

1. Peasant-style clothes from the '70s are back. You:

  a. run out and buy a smock top and a big peace sign poster for your room.

  b. think that it's just that—'70s clothes. This is the 21st century. Why would you wear something your mom probably wore?

  c. buy a cool flowing gauze skirt that you found at the thrift store and layer it with some of your more contemporary clothes.

2. Miss Popular gets a new shirt everyone just loves. You've had that same shirt in the back of your closet for a month, long before she got hers. You:

  a. gross out! Now you'll push it even farther back in your closet. You wouldn't think of wearing the same shirt as Miss Priss. Yuck!

  b. pull the shirt out, wash it, iron it, and wear it every other day.

  c. leave it in your closet until you decide you want to wear it. Who cares if she has the same shirt? You know you bought yours first.

3. A guy compliments you on your jacket. You reply:

  a. "Thanks."

b. "Yeah, whatever."

c. "Really? I bought it last month but never wore it. Then I lost it, but I found it in my little brother's room. I knew it was a totally cool jacket, so...."

4. **You find out from your older sis that the high school girls are wearing capris and cropped tees. You:**

a. cut the bottoms off all of your pants and buy ten cropped tops. Wait 'til your crew sees you now!

b. like the look, and go for it. But you'd also be equally happy to stay with a style all your own.

c. announce to your sis, "All your high school friends look like they've outgrown their pants and shirts. Tell them they really should buy clothes that fit."

5. **Overall, how would you describe your style?**

a. "I wear what I like and whatever's comfortable. If what I wear happens to be currently in style, then fine. I just wear whatever is cool to me."

b. "Whatever's cool at the moment, I am totally into it. You gotta have clothes that are in style!"

c. "I like comfortable clothes. People can think what they want of how I dress, but I don't care. I dress like me."

Scoring

Add up your points, and read on to see what your answers say about you.

1.	**a.** 3	**b.** 1	**c.** 2	**4.**	**a.** 3	**b.** 2	**c.** 1
2.	**a.** 1	**b.** 3	**c.** 2	**5.**	**a.** 2	**b.** 3	**c.** 1
3.	**a.** 2	**b.** 1	**c.** 3				

5–8 Points: STYLE SHOULDER SHRUGGER

You deserve a lot of credit. You aren't at all sucked in by this whole fad thing. You couldn't care less about what style's in and which one's out. That's really cool. Trends are so fickle anyway—one week something's the hottest thing, and the next week wearing it is a criminal offense! The only thing is, you need to make sure you respect yourself. You should pride yourself on your appearance. Don't get us wrong—taking pride in yourself doesn't mean you have to empty your piggy bank and run to the nearest mall to buy what's in. It just means you care about how you look, wearing the fad or not!

9–11 Points: **LOVELY LADY**

Good for you! You seem to have found the perfect balance of your own style. You have a unique attribute that most girls don't have. If you like what's in style, you wear it, but *only* if you like it. If you don't, you just stick with what you have or what you like. Who cares if it's trendy or if all the popular girls are wearing it? If you like it, you wear it…if you don't, you won't.

12–15 Points: **CHIC CHICK**

You're styling! You've got the look that's "in" and that's obviously important to you. Just one (OK maybe more than one) piece of advice: Use caution when it comes to trends, and don't stick yourself with a wardrobe you secretly hate. Just because certain clothes might be dubbed "the trend of the season," doesn't mean if you dislike the look that you aren't cool. And one more thing—just think how expensive it's gonna be to keep up with all the fads! Just be yourself, and everyone will like you because of who you are, not because of what you wear.

Chapter 6

Get a Grip

Everybody has a different approach to certain sitches. Who you are inside says a lot about how you deal with things like embarrassing moments, beating the boredom blues, managing the almighty dollar, and generally looking on the bright side.

How Well Do You Handle Embarrassing Situations?

Everybody has embarrassing moments, but it's how you recover from those sticky situations that makes all the difference. What's your style when it comes to recovering from those "I wanna crawl into a hole and disappear" moments? Do you get completely red-cheeked or are you oh-so savvy at saving face?

I. **You're walking across the street and your crush sees you trip over the curb and fall. You:**

a. blow it off. It doesn't matter if you're a klutz. If he really likes you, he won't care.

b. get up, giggle, and say, "I meant to do that."

c. pretend you are sick the next day and avoid him in the halls for the next two months.

2. **You're shopping with your mom and your crush sees you. You:**

a. make a fuss, pretending your mom's picking stuff out for herself.

b. duck behind a clothes rack and hope he didn't really see you.

c. casually continue as if he weren't there.

3. **You're daydreaming about your crush and accidentally walk into the boys' locker room. Your crush is standing there in his gym clothes. You:**

a. pretend you have amnesia and say, "Where am I? I'm confused."

b. turn beet-red and run into the wall on your way out.

c. stand there in a daze, and then giggle uncontrollably.

4. **You're chatting it up with your crush at the community swimming pool. As you're talking, you back up and fall right into the pool. You:**

a. come up sputtering for air in water that's only four feet deep (and you're five feet tall).

b. stand up and say, "I meant to do that."

101

c. jokingly pretend your friend pushed you, even though she's on the other side of the pool.

5. You're talking to your crush on the phone. Your brother puts you on speaker phone as your parents walk in the door. You:

a. hang up immediately and apologize to your crush the next day.

b. keep talking.

c. say something bizarre that you would never normally say just to give your brother a jolt.

6. You're in a parking lot, and your dad is singing a song from his generation. You:

a. sing along with him. You two always sing together.

b. duck behind the nearest car and pretend you're not with him.

c. continue walking with him, without saying a word.

7. You hop off the bus as your dad pulls up. He rolls down his window and shouts loudly, "Hi, Princess! How was your day, Sweetie?" You:

a. get back on the bus. This isn't your stop.

b. run home as fast as you can and pretend you don't know this weirdo.

c. yell back, "Hi, Dad! My day was *juuust* peachy!"

8. You're walking through the cafeteria, and everyone's giving you funny looks because there's a piece of toilet paper trailing behind you. You:

a. run into the bathroom and wait for the comfort of your friends.

b. pick it up and blow your nose.

c. say, "Hey, you never know when you're going to need it!"

9. It's the night of your first dance and, when your date arrives to pick you up, your dad says, "OK, kids, what should I wear to the dance tonight?" You:

a. run out the door, grabbing your date by the hand, and later pretend that your dad was your psycho uncle.

b. tell him your dad was repeatedly dropped on his head as a child.

c. make some introductions, and quickly leave.

10. **You're at the park and a gust of wind blows your dress up to your waist. You:**

a. hide under the slide.

b. quickly grab your skirt and hold it down.

c. run to the Porta-Potty and vow not to come out until after dark.

Scoring

Add up your points, and read on to see what your answers say about you.

1.	a. 1	b. 3	c. 2		**6.**	a. 3	b. 1	c. 2
2.	a. 2	b. 1	c. 3		**7.**	a. 1	b. 2	c. 3
3.	a. 3	b. 1	c. 2		**8.**	a. 1	b. 2	c. 3
4.	a. 1	b. 3	c. 2		**9.**	a. 1	b. 3	c. 2
5.	a. 3	b. 2	c. 1		**10.**	a. 2	b. 3	c. 1

10–14 Points: You're QUEEN FREAK-OUT

You are easily embarrassed. You need to realize that when you freak out over an embarrassing situation, you only draw more attention to yourself. Don't let the little mishaps in life get you down. Learn to laugh at yourself, and you'll feel tons better. Promise.

15–19 Points: You're LADY LIGHTEN-UP

You are easily embarrassed and don't recover from embarrassing situations very well. You need some work in lightening up. Don't take stuff so seriously. You slipped in the hallway in front of your crush? So what? Pick yourself up, dust yourself off, and move on with confidence.

20–24 Points: You're MISS MASK-IT-UP

You're doing OK, but you could use a little work in the saving-face department. Since it doesn't come all that naturally, keep practicing. You'll be a pro at handling embarrassing situations in no time flat.

25–30 Points: You're PRINCESS COVER-UP

You can cover up a bad situation quickly and humorously. You might not always have the best saves, but it doesn't matter because you're not that easily embarrassed. You're comfy with who you are, and that's all that matters. Congrats!

Can You Read Your Palm?

Over many centuries, patterns have been noticed in the palm that can reveal your talents, emotional nature, and the way you approach situations in life. Look at the palm on the hand that you write with—that one has the most energy in it.

Fate Line

The Fate Line starts at the base of your hand, near your wrist, and extends to one of your fingers. It's said to show the direction of your natural talents and interests. By figuring out what your Fate Line is telling you, you can gain clues about what line of study, or which career might be a good choice for you.

The Fate Line heads toward your index finger

If your Fate Line points in the direction of your index, or "Jupiter," finger, you have a talent for things like science, math, and numbers. You are good at measuring things and have a real gift for following a procedure step by step. You could succeed in fields like medicine, veterinary science, biology, or accounting.

The Fate Line heads toward your middle finger

If your Fate Line points in the direction of your middle, or "Saturn," finger, you are determined to do things your own way. People with this line often create their own paths in life, starting their own businesses or promoting their talents in a unique way. You tend to be a leader rather than a follower.

The Fate Line heads toward your ring finger

If your Fate Line points in the direction of your ring, or "Apollo," finger, you may become famous! This line is pretty rare. If you have this line, at some point in your life you might end up in the newspaper or on TV. Your accomplishments could be in any field. Just remember: Don't let all that attention go to your head!

The Fate Line heads toward your pinkie

If your Fate Line points in the direction of your pinkie, or "Mercury," finger, you are a born communicator. Writing, public speaking, or performing is your thing. You are great with words, and you find it easy to express yourself. You could become a stand-up comedian, an actor, a journalist, or a college professor.

The Heart Line

The Heart Line, beginning near your pinkie, shows your emotional nature. Are you an optimist, pessimist, or somewhere in between? Your Heart Line will reveal the true you.

The Heart Line slopes upward

When your Heart Line slopes upward, it shows that you have a positive outlook on life. Even when something weird happens to you, you see it as a challenge, not a disaster. You have a "can do" attitude that lifts up other people.

Heart Line ends in a straight line

You are a mixture of optimism and pessimism, depending on the situation. Overall, you are pretty easy-going. You don't like to stand out in a crowd, and prefer to test the vibes before you make a move.

The Heart Line slopes downward

You get discouraged way too easily. Work at overcoming that pessimism and embracing a more positive attitude. You need to reprogram yourself. If you stick to it, you'll even see physical changes in your palm. Over months, the line on your hand might start to move upward. (Yes, the lines in the palm *do* change over time!)

The Life Line

Your Life Line runs between your thumb and index finger, down to the base of your hand.

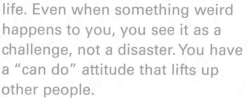

A Fun Way to Learn More About You

The Life Line has a break or a split

Contrary to myth, if your Life Line has a split or a break in the middle, that doesn't mean you are destined for an early death! Breaks in the Life Line indicate a big turning point in your life, such as a change in residence, a new relationship, or a fresh career.

The Life Line is doubled

Double Life Lines are rare, and they always mean that you have two distinct sides to your personality. The trick is to find a way to express both of these "selves" in your daily life. This can be quite a challenge.

Special Markings

Some people have rare lines in their palms that not everybody has. That's what makes 'em special!

The Mystic Cross

"La Croix Mystique" is what it's called when an X marks the spot below the Heart Line. It is seen as a special sign, one that shows  extra intuition and psychic ability. If you have this marking, you can often see one step ahead of things, gaining glimpses of the future in your dreams or daydreams. You are great at "reading" people. You usually know if somebody is being truthful!

The Ring of Solomon

If you have The Ring of Solomon, a small line dipping just below the crease in your index finger, you are the thoughtful type, always trying to figure out what makes people tick. You are drawn to philosophy, psychology, and the arts. There's nothing you like better than sitting and pondering the meaning of life!

The Girdle of Venus

If you have double lines etched under the creases of your middle and ring fingers, you might have lots of drama in your personal life. Relationships tend to be like something out of a movie, with big scenes and lots of emotion. Since you find all of this melodrama exciting, maybe you should become an actor!

quiz

What Makes You Totally Bored?

You're uttering those two dismal words: "I'm bored." What are you gonna do if you're not even sure what's making you restless? Take this quiz to find out exactly what your psyche is craving when you feel a case of the snores coming on. Hey, it'll give you something to do for a while anyway. Reading cereal boxes and organizing your CDs is getting old fast!

l. Rainy weather that lasts for days makes you:

a. give in to the little girl next door who's been begging you to play dominoes.

b. decide to take on some crossword puzzles.

c. use the sleep sofa as a trampoline.

d. sink into your inflatable chair.

2. Sentenced to an hour in your room, you fantasize about:

a. having your buds over for a huge slumber party.

b. being an undercover agent.

c. swimming twenty laps in the rec center pool.

d. eating a double chocolate-dipped doughnut.

3. You've been moping around the house all day when Mom says, "Find something constructive to do—or clean the basement." You:

a. call up every single person in your phone book, even Aunt Gladys.

b. create a fabulous new way to make fruit-flavored ice cubes.

107

c. invent a game called Crumpled Tissue B-ball with your brother.

d. say, "Forget it, I'm too tired," and then get relegated to the basement, where you do a weak clean-up job.

4. **When your friend invites you to spend the weekend with her, you:**

   a. ask if you can stay the week.

   b. pack all your jewelry-making supplies so you guys can make each other matching earrings and necklaces.

   c. put new bearings on your in-line skates—you'll be needing them!

   d. bring along a library of tear-jerk movies and a box of tissues.

5. **Your parents say you have to go along with them on a business trip, so you:**

a. ask to invite your three best friends to go, too.

b. bring along your laptop.

c. sign up for daily karate classes at the hotel's gym.

d. buy a boxed set of meditation tapes.

6. **When the family you baby-sit for tells you they're going away for three weeks this summer, you:**

   a. ask them if they need a sitter to go along.

   b. decide to open a lemonade stand on your front lawn to earn the extra bucks you'll be missing out on.

   c. plan to take some daylong bicycle trips.

   d. listen to depressing music while reading *The Diary of Anne Frank* for the fifth time.

Scoring

Review your answers, and total up how many of each letter you selected. Then, look up the letter that you chose most, and see what your answers reveal about you!

Mostly A's: ONLY THE LONELY

Chances are you're friendly and outgoing—the kind of person your buds enjoy hanging with. You're a girl who is happiest around people and you thrive on interacting with others. If you get bored when flying solo, what you might actually be feeling is loneliness.

Bustin' Boredom: Think about enrolling in an after-school program where you'd be surrounded by other girls (and boys). Or, organize time to get together with friends you know from school or friends you don't get to see often, such as those who live in other towns or that you met during summer programs. A visit to see cousins or grandparents can also be a bright spot during boring weekends. When in-person visits are impossible, you can always rely on the good ol' phone to connect you with others. And if you're online, you can keep in touch with lots of people. Try to keep things in a healthy balance, however. Since you will surely find yourself alone for stretches at some points in your life, learn to enjoy your own company. It can be rejuvenating to have some solitude or down time.

Mostly B's: MIND TRIPPER

You're a girl who thrives on mental challenges. You get bored when days are long, and stimulation is short. Sitting around for days on end is definitely not for you. It's not that you *can't* relax, but too much lazing around makes you feel like your mind is turning to mush.

Bustin' Boredom: To feel better, rev up your gray matter. Think about all the times you've said to yourself, "I wish I could do that, but I don't have time." There's no better time to tackle a goal than when you're bored! Make a list of some things you'd like to do. Set reasonable goals that'll be fun, and don't freak if you don't get to all of them—after all, it's not like you're being graded or anything. If you're a serious reader, dig into that five-hundred page novel that's been sitting on your shelf. Get a cool 3-D puzzle you can set up on a spare table and work on it whenever you want. Why not learn how to bake a delicious chocolate cake, make origami figures, or even conquer fractions once and for all? Whatever you do, you'll enjoy it that much more when you're inspired.

Mostly C's: ON-THE-GO GIRL

You probably chose so many C responses because they're active. You're the sort of girl who gets bored when confined to small spaces or unable to move freely. Even the thought of a long car ride brings on hives—and days indoors are definitely not your thing. You need physical challenges. Exercising your muscles makes you feel good. You also thrive on competition—either with others or yourself.

Bustin' Boredom: It's no wonder that being on the go rids you of boredom—it releases those feel-good neural hormones called *endorphins*. So, when the weather's right, make sure you do all the things you love—hiking, fishing, jogging. And muster up the courage to try new sports, such as rock climbing. Set some goals for yourself, such as increasing your stamina, improving your tennis serve, finding out what yoga is all about, or earning your next swim badge. When the sun's not shining, grab your umbrella and take a walk in the rain. Or, get into an indoor activity, such as mini-basketball, Foosball, or Ping-Pong. If you're by yourself, no prob. Try an exercise tape, hit a tennis ball against the basement or garage wall, or learn to juggle. Still yawning? Volunteer to do some yard work. Your mom will fall over!

Mostly D's: DESPERADO

You might enjoy being alone sometimes, and that's OK. But, you could be isolating yourself by moping or being down. Lots of girls say they're bored when what they're really feeling is lonely or unsure. When you find the comfort of your bedspread appealing for hours on end, you might be trying to make yourself feel better when troubling emotions are bubbling under the surface.

Bustin' Boredom: If you don't recognize your feelings or can't express them appropriately, you might be zoning out. If your boredom is really sadness or worry, figure out what's causing it so you can do something about it and move on. When you find yourself in a bad mood, try talking to a treasured friend, writing in your journal, or simply letting your thoughts wander to discover what's on your mind. If you can't figure out what's bothering you, ask a parent or other trusted adult for help. Hopefully, you'll find a way to deal with whatever's getting to you. And then you'll be interested in stepping outside your bedroom door to discover all the other awesome things there are to do.

USE YOUR TIME WISELY!

No matter what's causing your boredom, volunteering your time to help others is a great way to get out of the house, meet and work with other people, and stimulate your brain. Choose an activity that best suits the unique needs you discovered above. Check your local paper to see what possibilities exist.

- If you like being with people, you might lead a library story hour for toddlers, help out with after-school day care, or work in a soup kitchen.

- If you like mental challenges, you can try making touch-books for blind children, training pets at the pound,

or offering your time at a candidate's headquarters.

- Physically oriented girls can help the elderly with chores, coach a younger sib's swim team, or pitch in on community clean-up days.

- When girls are going through a particularly hard time, they often find that volunteering for those less fortunate makes them feel better. See if you can collect toys or books for pediatric units at the local hospital, or visit sick children.

Whatever you choose, be sure you think about doing at least one thing to make each day satisfying or memorable.

Can You Talk to Animals?

You've seen animals all around you—in your yard, in the park, or maybe when you were away with your family on vacation. But did you know that each animal you see carries a special meaning? Many people, including Native Americans, believe that animals are special helpers—kind of like furry guardian angels. They look out for you, and bring blessings and good luck. Different animals deliver different messages. By learning what each animal means, you can figure out what they could be telling you when you see them in the wild.

Here's a list of traditional animals and what it means when you see them. Keep in mind that an animal is only a special messenger if it is a wild animal. Pets or animals that live in zoos don't count!

Robins

Robins not only show that spring is coming, but they bring good luck to the person who sees them. When you see a robin, expect something new to enter your life. This could be a new friend or boyfriend, or an idea for a new creative project.

Lizards

Not everybody appreciates lizards, but like all animals, they carry  meaning when you see them. When you spot a lizard, be on the lookout for events from the past to get stirred up again. You could bump into an old classmate or hear from an ex-friend— which could be weird or cool— depending on the situation.

Blue Jays

Blue jays are noisy and talkative. They always seem to be complaining about something. Although they are pretty birds, with those blue feathers, they signify that some sort of conflict is coming. Try not to lose your temper over minor things, because you don't want to be caught in an argument. If you're careful, you can avoid getting into trouble.

Rabbits

Rabbits show that your ideas are taking root. Things that you are planning, like getting good grades, working on a relationship, or redecorating your room should all become easier when a rabbit is around. If a rabbit decides to live in your yard or garden, this is a good thing, although your parents might not want it around eating your vegetables!

Spiders

It's easy to get freaked out when you see a spider, but they are rarely dangerous, and are actually a good sign. Think about how the spider works hard to make a beautiful web. No other animal builds a house so pretty! The spider tells you that your creativity will be flowing, and this is a positive thing.

Deer

Deer always tell you that it's time to spend more time outdoors. Sometimes it's tempting to just watch TV or stay inside playing video games. Deer tell you to take better care of your body, by eating the right foods or exercising more. If you do, you'll be feeling more energized in no time.

Frogs or Toads

Frogs and toads both mean that you need to take some quiet time so that you can figure things out in your life. Maybe you need to get over a fight you had with someone, and it would be better to cool your temper before you talk to the person again. Or maybe you would like to write some thoughts or poems down in a journal just for fun. Quiet time can make you feel much better about things.

Hawks

Hawks are very positive messengers. They are a traditional sign of wisdom and good luck to Native Americans, and they can be good for you, too! Whenever you watch a hawk, seeing its calm, beautiful flight, your spirits are lifted. The hawk tells you to trust your heart and listen to your intuition—especially if you have to make an important decision about something. If you look deep inside yourself, the answers will become clear to you.

Foxes

The bushy fox carries an interesting meaning. It can warn you not to be fooled by appearances. Somebody could be trying to impress you—only he or she might not be a good person. It's important to look deeper into things after you've seen a fox. A fox tells you to look out for yourself and to make sure that a friend is treating you right!

Butterflies

Butterflies are always positive signs. They mean that you have the ability to connect with the energy of dreams and good luck. If you see a butterfly, you might experience something exciting during the next few weeks. You could discover that somebody cute has a crush on you. Or you could receive recognition for your talents or your hard work.

Ladybugs

Ladybugs emit a curious and playful energy. When ladybugs are around, they are reminding you that you need to have more fun. If a ladybug gets into your house and shows up in your room, it is sending an especially strong message that it's time for you to lighten up! Reach out to friends and loved ones who always put a smile on your face, and share some laughs with them.

A Fun Way to Learn More About You

Do You Have Money Moxie?

Some girls are just naturally good at dealing with the almighty dollar. Others can't hang on to a single slippery dime. Does money make you panic or are you a major saver? Take this quick money management quiz, and then match your answers to each question with the real-life advice that follows on how to max your cash.

How You Spend

You *had* to have those killer new platform clogs. You,

    a. were desperate, so you paid $60 more to get the designer version you found in a department store.

    b. went to the knock-off, cheapie shoe store and found a pair that look just as cool for $25.

If you picked **a**, you're a **Silly Spender**. When you want something, you have to have it yesterday! Here are a few pointers for you.

1. *Push yourself to be patient.* You're the girl who's *gotta have* that new mini to survive. Hold up! Sneak a peek at what you're spending and wait a month for your favorite style to go on sale.

2. *Stop spending spontaneously.* You saw those clogs and you bought them on the spot. It felt like you'd die if you didn't spend. But they're not worth the money if you can't go for pizza with pals because you spent all your dough.

3. *Shop around for better deals.* You might find a better deal if you take a sec to look somewhere else. Besides, think of all the awesome things you could've done with that extra $35! A new sweater or pair of jeans could be yours—and would look great with the knock-off clogs.

If you picked **b**, you're **Perfect with Pennies.** You pinch pennies well. In fact, someone in your family probably taught you to be thrifty with your money. Here are some ways to save a little more!

114

1. *Put away the money you save.*
OK, you realize you saved $35 hunting around for cheaper clogs. Now feed some of it to your piggy bank, or stick the money in a savings account!

2. *Buy some stuff at the thrift shop.*
You always scope for cheap goodies in stores. How about hitting places where the stuff's always on sale? You can find stylin' jeans for dirt-cheap!

3. *Buy something fun for yourself.*
Yep, we're giving you permission. You're so careful with money that you rarely splurge. And, when you actually do, you feel guilty. Don't. Every so often, it's perfectly OK.

How You Save

Your birthday was way happy for you! Along with a sack of sweet presents, you raked in $100. You:

> **a.** took the money to the mall! Yippee!
>
> **b.** took the money to the bank. Hooray!

If you picked **a**, you're a **Sorry Saver**. No one can pass up a good shopping spree. But you're basically minus in the savings department. Read on.

1. *Save a tiny stash of cash.*
If you've never saved money, it's not like you'll be able to chuck the whole $100 in the bank. So, start small. Tuck a few bucks under your bed every time you baby-sit or have a birthday.

You'll have a little savings faster than you can get the money to the mall!

2. *Get a real savings account.*
You know the place that cashes checks and has one of those machines that spits out bucks? It's called a bank. And it's a good idea for you to put your money there. Just think—if you put in $1 every week, you'll have $52 in a year.

3. *Don't blow your money in one big shopping spree.*
Slow down. One hundred smackers is a lot of money. Don't slap it down all in one place—or in one day. Spending it little by little works best, and allows for emergency situations. Don't you need those new sneaks soon anyway?

If you picked **b**, you're a **Super Saver**. You'd save gum wrappers if they were worth a penny. Here are a few more tips on how to save money.

1. *Look into a checking account.* You're so good with money, you might as well start establishing awesome credit history now. (A savings account wouldn't hurt, either, but you probably already have one!) You might need a college loan when you're older. Or, maybe a car. If a bank has done business with you for a few years, they're more likely to let you borrow some bucks. Ask a parent to help you get started.

2. *Ask your parents for more cash.* If they're into saving money, ask your folks if they'll consider putting you on a "matching program." That means for every dollar you put into your piggy, they'll match it, by putting in a dollar more. If the 'rents say no, see if they'll put in even a quarter for every dollar. Hey, it's worth asking!

3. *Invest your stash.* You really *can* do it right now. Buy things that are likely to be worth money later, like baseball cards or antique dolls. And if you want to invest in stocks, that's a possibility, too. Write to companies, like McDonald's and Disney, and tell them you're a kid and want to buy just one share. Usually, they'll sell it to you.

How You Bring in a Buck of Your Own

You're low on dough and completely desperate. If you don't score more money soon, you'll *never* have those new swim goggles you need. You:

   a. ask for a big fat raise in your allowance.

   b. see if the lady you baby-sit for will tell her friends about you.

If you picked **a**, you're a **Buck Beggar**. Sheesh, the least you deserve is a bigger allowance, right? *Wrong.* Your 'rents aren't made of cash. Here are some things to do instead.

1. *Make money on your own.* If you can mow a lawn, shovel snow, or take out people's trash, you can make moolah. Ask people around the neighborhood if they need help with odd jobs. If you see little kids around, ask about being their baby-sitter.

2. *Stop asking for so much money.* Handouts are the easiest way to get a quick buck. But don't make parents mad by begging for extra dough. If you have to ask, offer to do more chores to earn some money.

3. *Stop spending so much, period.* If you didn't spend, you wouldn't need so much of a raise. Cut back on the candy, and other things you can live without.

If you picked **b**, you're **Bringin' in the Bacon**. If anyone needs a hand, you're there to lend it—for a price. Business means bucks, so here's what to do to make a few more.

1. *Work at home.*
Your parents know you're a worker and might be willing to give you more responsibilities. Offer to do the laundry or walk the dog for a raise.

2. *Be realistic.*
You only have two hands, and they don't need to work all the time! It's fine to take on more baby-sitting jobs as long as you can handle your homework. Don't feel bad if you have to turn down a job. Your personal life is important, too!

3. *Keep up the good work!*
Dealing with your money isn't your major malfunction. So don't change too much. You're already awesome with your bucks!

GO AHEAD! BREAK THAT PIGGY BANK!

Put all of your money into a real savings account. Here's how:

1. Make sure the bank doesn't charge a monthly fee for your savings account. And check to see if a minimum deposit is required. You should be able to get a free student account without any trouble.

2. Some banks charge a fee if you don't deposit money every month. And they don't always tell you that when you open your account. Find a place that won't charge you. After all, there will be months (like around the holidays) when it just seems impossible to save.

3. Ask a bank employee if there are any penalties for withdrawing your dough. Try to find a bank that lets you withdraw without charging you to do so.

Can You Pass the Anti-Pessimist Test?

Ever been around someone who's constantly expecting disaster? She probably has a pessimistic attitude a mile wide. While an optimist sees the doughnut, a pessimist sees the hole. Which are you? Take this quiz to find out—and learn how to defect to the Optimists Club, if you are a pessimist.

1. **You're running out the door to catch the bus. As the door slams behind you, Mom calls out, "There's something we need to talk about when you get home!" Your first thought is:**

   a. that she's finally letting you have that huge sleepover you've been asking about!

   b. about a first-period math test you've been worrying about.

   c. "Uh-oh!" You're in serious trouble.

2. **You've been acting in community theater since third grade. After your big audition for the spring musical, the director asks to see you privately before she announces the cast. You imagine:**

   a. your audition blew her away and you've landed the lead, for sure.

   b. that she probably needs you to read the script one more time so she can decide which part best suits you.

   c. that you blew your audition. Rather than up the humiliation factor, she wants to tell you in private that you did not get a role.

3. **You and your family are going camping for the first time. You:**

   a. can't wait! What could be better than roasting S'mores over a campfire and sleeping under the stars every night?

   b. are a little worried about not having running water for five straight days, but at least it's something different to do.

   c. can't stop thinking about bears and poison ivy.

4. You take your brand-new kitty to the vet for her first shots and checkup. When the vet calls your house the next day, you assume:

a. he's gonna give you a discount on pet insurance!

b. he probably just wants to let you know when you need to bring your kitty back for booster shots.

c. he's calling to tell you that your adorable little bundle of fur is very sick. You just *knew* this kitten was too good to be true.

5. You find a $5 bill on the floor in the mall's food court. The person who dropped it is obviously long gone. You immediately think:

a. "Yes! Now I can get those drop earrings I've been eyeing."

b. "Guess I can use this for lunch money next week."

c. "How come I never find $20 bills?"

6. It's finally summer vacation and your BFF has invited you to spend a few days at her fam's beach house. You just *know* that:

a. the sun will definitely be shining on you and your BFF! You're packing nothing but shorts and sunscreen!

b. even if it rains the entire time, it won't totally sink your plans. You have tons of gossip to catch up on.

c. something *horrible* will happen. Last time you went away, you got sun poisoning the first day.

7. The coolest store in the mall is having an incredible contest. You can win backstage passes to see Avril Lavigne in concert—just enough passes for you and three of your best buds! You quickly:

a. fill out the entry form and start picking out a tie—you just *know* you'll win.

b. enter the contest. Why not? You probably won't win, but it's worth a shot.

c. walk out of the store without entering. You never win anything, so why bother?

8. You just got invited to a sleep-over with an awesome celestial theme. You:

a. are jazzed! The weekend can't come soon enough—it's gonna be unbelievable!

b. figure it'll be fun—if your mom will let you go (you've been slacking on chores lately) and you don't fall asleep at 11 p.m. like you did last time.

c. know this girl's strict parents are going to ruin the whole thing, so why bother going? You should just stay home and watch reruns instead.

9. Your English teacher announces he's reading *your* story aloud to the entire class as an example. Your first thought is:

a. "This is totally cool!" You know he's holding your story up as a model of creativity, wit, and talent!

b. that he needs to kill a few minutes of class time, and your story just happened to be on the top of the pile.

c. "Could it really be so bad that he feels compelled to single it out as an example of what *not* to do?" You vow never to write another thing for his class.

10. It's Friday night. At the last minute, your BFF wants to rush out to see that hot new movie that just opened. If you leave right away, you might make it before the film starts. You decide to:

a. go for it! You'll probably be able to just walk right in since everyone else will already be seated!

b. go if she really wants to. Either you'll get in or you won't. So what?

c. forget it! The tickets will definitely be sold out.

Scoring

Review your answers, and total up the number of each letter you chose. Then read below to see what your answers reveal about you!

Mostly A's: OPTIMISTIC POWER

You see the best and expect the best—and often that's what you get! That's good, because optimistic people tend to be happier and healthier than those with negative perspectives. You're a people magnet, too. You undoubtedly have a great circle of buds who love basking in the glow of your happy thoughts. Just make sure you don't get *so* optimistic that you refuse to acknowledge life's bitter moments. If your best bud is devastated over her parents' divorce, it won't help her to hear that *you* think it's a great idea. In other words, be happy but be *real.* Watch those unrealistic expectations, too—they can set you up for major let-downs. Expecting to ace a test you didn't study for isn't optimistic thinking— it's dreaming! Continue to enjoy all the good you see in life, but don't be afraid to acknowledge the drags either. It's the total life package that makes it all exciting!

Mostly B's: HO-HUMMING ALONG

You see things for what they are and just seem to go with the flow. This even keel keeps you moving, yet you might sometimes miss the point. Life is filled with ups and downs—and sometimes you've just got to enjoy the ride! It can be great to play it safe—you don't drive anyone crazy with your endless grins or hopeless doldrums. But instead of waking up expecting to just coast through another day, pause for a minute to tell yourself that it's going to be a *great* day! Think about something terrific in your life (that new crush?), or in your day (the Spanish test you just know you're going to ace). Don't be afraid to expect a bit more out of life—you just might get it!

Mostly C's: PERSISTENTLY PESSIMISTIC

You definitely need to pull back the curtains and let some sun shine in—you've been living in the dark, girl! Stop anticipating the worst. It's funny how life has a habit of living up (or down!) to our expectations. Never underestimate the power of positive thinking and personal pep-talking. Look at it this way—what have you got to lose, except for a bum outlook? Careful, because you could also drive people away if you keep up with your persistent negativity. So turn the negative 'tude around and look for that silver lining. Odds are good that you're going to find life is a whole lot happier than you thought!

See Ya!

That's it—secret's out. By now, you should know your secret self *sooo* well. And while you're made up of more than multiple choice questions, your quiz scores should have shed some major light on all those great traits that add up to YOU! Who you are, why you do the things you do, and how you can take your already awesome qualities and make them even better.

Plus, for further self-enlightenment, you now know how to really read your handwriting, why red (or blue or pink or purple) is more than just a color, and what all those lines and creases in your palm predict about your life (no crystal ball required). Hope you had a blast getting better acquainted with the true you. No need to be a stranger to yourself, is there?

Credits

When we first had the idea for *The Girls' Life Big Book of Quizzes: Your Secret Self Revealed!,* I don't think we had a clue what we were getting ourselves into. After putting out *GL* for nine years, we had so many great quizzes and info to share with you, we hardly knew how to pack it all in. But, what you are holding in your hands is the best of the best.

I would like to give a hearty thanks to those whose talents made this book—and who make *GL*—great. As they say, behind every great magazine is a super talented team of editors, writers, and designers. And, for the past nine years, *GL* has been lucky enough to have some of the best. Thanks a million to executive editor Kelly White, Chun Kim, Sarah Cordi, Georgia Wilson, and Debbie Chaillou. And thanks, too, to the great folks at Scholastic. We never could've done this without you.

Writing Credits

Chapter 1: *Do You Have a Positive Outlook?* (Laura Sandler), *What's Your Gotta-Have-Fun Style?* (Lisa Mulcahy), *Where Do You Fall in the Chinese Zodiac?* (Jennifer Shepherd), *How Motivated Are You?* (Lisa Mulcahy), *Is Your Number Up?* (Jennifer Shepherd)

Chapter 2: *Are You a Loyal Friend?* (Marie Therese Miller), *What's Your Birth Order?* (Roni-Cohen Sandler), *Do You Give Fab Friend Advice?* (Jenny B. Davis), *What's Your Dependability Vibe?* (Lisa Mulcahy)

Chapter 3: *Who's Your Dream Dude?* (Lisa Mulcahy), *What's Your Sign?* (Kelly White), *What's Your Gabbing-With-Guys Groove?* (Jennifer Pangyanszki), *Can You Crack the Crush Code?* (Gabrielle L. Gabrielle), *Are You Starstruck?* (Lori A. McDonald)

Chapter 4: *What Kind of Smart Are You?* (Jennifer Burton Bauer), *Do You Know How to Analyze Your Handwriting?* (Jennifer Shepherd), *Are You Fit for Gym Survival?* (Michelle Silver), *What's Your Class Clown Status?* (Michelle Silver)

Chapter 5: *How Far Would You Go to Be Popular?* (Keren Katz and Mandy Ginzburg), *What's Your Favorite Color?* (Jennifer Shepherd), *Is Your Style Totally Unique?* (C.L. Herren)

Chapter 6: *How Well Do You Handle Embarrassing Situations?* (Jaime Engel and Clarissa Hartl), *Can You Read Your Palm?* (Jennifer Shepherd), *What Makes You Totally Bored?* (Roni Cohen-Sandler), *Can You Talk to Animals?* (Jennifer Shepherd), *Do You Have Money Moxie?* (Kristen Kemp)